INFORMATION THEORY

An Introduction for Scientists and Engineers

D1528143

INFORMATION THEORY

An Introduction for Scientists and Engineers

GORDON RAISBECK

The M. I. T. Press

Massachusetts Institute of Technology, Cambridge, Massachusetts

4
365
.R3

Dedicated to

Professor George Polya

who taught me that mathematics can be entertaining

Preface

The object of this book is to explain some of the ideas in modern information theory and to show how they can be applied to certain problems in signal transmission and signal detection. It is not intended as a text or reference work. It evolved from several sets of lectures at various times and places to audiences of scientists and engineers who had no specialized knowledge of communications or information theory. The earliest sections, which introduce the fundamental ideas of amount of information and channel capacity, may nevertheless be of interest to readers with less technical background.

I thank the Institute for Defense Analyses for permission to use herein portions of IDA Technical Note 60-19, "Modulation, Coding and Information Theory," which was written with the support of Contract NOSD-50 with the Advance Research Projects Agency; the U.S. Navy Bureau of Ships for permission to use herein portions of Project TRIDENT Technical Report 1291262, "An Introduction to Modulation, Coding, Information Theory, and Detection," which was written with the support of Contract Nobsr 81564; my colleagues J. Kaiser, G. Sutton, and others at IDA, who heard and criticized a series of lectures on which the Technical Note was based; my colleagues at Bell Telephone Laboratories, Inc., and Arthur D. Little, Inc., who likewise criticized subsequent oral presentations; Hugh Leney, M. S. Klein, P. B. Coggins, and Magnus Moll of Arthur D. Little, Inc., and Professor John M. Wozencraft of Massachusetts Institute of Technology, who read and criticized the manuscript; Claude E. Shannon, E. N. Gilbert, J. R. Pierce, C. C. Cutler, R. M. Fano, and others from whose publications I have borrowed liberally; and Mrs. Barbara Gibbons, who drew the figures.

GORDON RAISBECK

Cambridge, Massachusetts
September, 1963

Contents

3

Channel Capacity

4

Detection as a Communication Process

5

Coherent and Incoherent Integration

6

INFORMATION THEORY

An Introduction for Scientists and Engineers

1

A Definition of Information*

1.1   Why a New Definition?

Some paradoxes and misunderstandings about information have
arisen in recent years as the science of *information theory* has been
disseminated. The first misunderstanding is the belief that any
intelligent person ought to know what the word information means.

In any specialized study, new concepts arise that must have
names. Sometimes we name the concept after a person: Doppler
shift, Planck's constant. Sometimes we give it a number or letter:

---

* Many of the ideas of this chapter are adapted from E. N. Gilbert, "An
Outline of Information Theory," *Am. Statistician*, *12*, 13–19 (February, 1958).

the first law of thermodynamics, X-rays. Sometimes we make up a new word: meson, radio. But often we use a common word: current, mass.

When a new technical concept is named with a common word, the word acquires a new meaning. It is impossible to use the word in a technical context until that new meaning has been defined. *Pressing a suit* does not mean the same thing to a lawyer that it does to a tailor. And information does not mean the same thing to a communications engineer that it does to a police detective. There is no reason to expect anyone to know what the word information means to an information theorist unless he has been told.

In this book, we shall give the information theorist's definition of information, and some examples of how the word is used in its technical sense. In this way, we shall indicate why the concept is useful enough to be worth a name of its own, and attempt to show that the concept has enough in common with a nontechnical idea of information that no real violence is done to the language in appropriating this word to name it. Then we shall use the new concept as a tool to investigate the properties of certain communication systems and detection systems.

It is possible simply to state a mathematical definition of information, and proceed to demonstrate some of its properties. However, such an approach is likely to be unconvincing, because the definition itself does not indicate just why it was chosen. As an alternative, we shall discuss some reasonable and useful properties which we can hope a new definition of information will have, and use them to narrow down the search.

1.2   A Generalized Communication System

A generalized communication system is illustrated in Figure 1.1. The first element of this system is an *information source*. Although we have not yet defined what we mean by information, assume that the information source is a person talking. The output of the information source is called a *message*. If the information source is a person talking, the message is what he says.

The next element in the communication system is a *transmitter*. The transmitter transforms the message in some way and produces a signal suitable for transmission over the next element of this system, the communication *channel*. The input to the transmitter is the message, and the output of the transmitter is the *signal*. If the *transmitter* is a telephone handset, the *signal* is an electrical current proportional to the pressure of the sound waves impinging on the mouthpiece of the instrument.

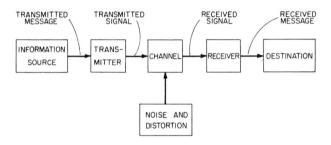

Figure 1.1   A generalized communication system.

The next element of this communication system is the *channel*. This is the medium used to transmit the signal from the transmitter to the receiver. While going through the channel, the signal may be altered by noise or distortion. In principle, *noise* and *distortion* may be differentiated on the basis that distortion is a fixed operation applied to the signal, while noise involves statistical and unpredictable perturbations. All or part of the effect of distortion can be corrected by applying the inverse operation or a partial inverse operation, but a perturbation due to noise cannot always be removed, because the signal does not always undergo the same change during transmission. In practice, the gamut of perturbation runs from noise to distortion. The input to the channel is the signal, sometimes called the transmitted signal. The output of the channel is the *received signal*, supposed to be in some sense a faithful representation of the transmitted signal.

The next element in this idealized communication system is the *receiver*. This operates on the received signal and attempts to reproduce from it the original message. It will ordinarily perform an operation which is approximately the inverse of the operation performed by the transmitter. The two operations may differ somewhat, however, because the receiver may also be required to combat the noise and distortion in the channel. The input to the receiver is the received signal, and the output of the receiver is the *received message*.

The last element of this communication system is the *destination*. This is the person or thing for whom the message is intended.

1.3   Information Defined in Mathematical Terms

An intuitively and aesthetically desirable definition of amount of information will be a measure of time or cost of transmitting messages. When applied to a message source, the definition will give us a measure of the cost or time required to send the output of the message source to the destination. When applied to a channel, in the form *information capacity of a channel*, it will give a measure of how long it takes to transmit the message generated by one message source, or of how many message sources can be accommodated by one channel. We should like to be able to say that two comparable information sources generate twice as much information as one, and that two comparable transmission channels could transmit twice as much information as one.

The moment we identify information with the cost or the time which it takes to transmit a message from a message source to a destination an interesting new fact emerges: Information is not so much a property of an individual message as it is a property of the whole experimental situation which produces the messages. For example, such utterances as: "How are you?," "Glad to meet you," "Happy birthday," "Congratulations on the birth of your child," "Best Wishes to Mother on Mother's Day," carry very little information. These phrases belong to a very small set of polite stereotyped utterances, normally used in certain stereotyped circumstances. The telegraph company has taken advantage of this fact by listing on its telegraph blanks some .100 stereotyped messages for use in appropriate stereotyped situations. The customer chooses a message, and the signal transmitted by the telegraph company contains only the few symbols necessary to identify the particular message which has been chosen. At the receiving office, a clerk reconstitutes the stereotyped message for transmission to the destination. The fact that such a stereotyped message contains less information than most utterances containing the same number of words is reflected in the lower cost to send such a message.

In order to get an effective definition of information, then, we shall consider not only the message generated or transmitted, but also the set of all messages of which the one chosen is a member. The message source may be considered as an experimental setup capable of producing many different outcomes at different times or under different stimuli, and the messages as the outcome of one particular experiment. If the possible messages form a set of a finite number of distinct entities, like English words, the source is called a discrete source. If the possible messages form a set in which individual members can differ minutely, like acoustic waves at a telephone, the source is called a continuous source. These categories are not exhaustive, but comprise most cases of practical interest.

"EXPERIMENT X"

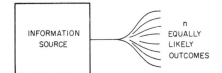

INFORMATION SOURCE

n EQUALLY LIKELY OUTCOMES

Figure 1.2   An idealized information source.

Consider an experiment X whose outcome is to be transmitted (see Figure 1.2). We will be particularly interested in cases in which the outcome of experiment X is an honest message, say written English or a television picture, but for the moment let us consider experiments in general. First of all, suppose experiment X has n equally likely outcomes. In this special case the definition of information evolves naturally from the following argument.

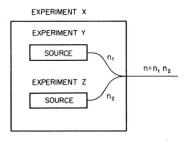

Figure 1.3   Two information sources combined into one.

The information in the message about X will be some function $f(n)$. Suppose X is a compound experiment (see Figure 1.3) consisting of two independent experiments Y and Z, which have n_1 and n_2 equally likely outcomes. The total number of outcomes of the compound experiment is the product of n_1 and n_2. Transmitting the outcome of X is equivalent to transmitting the outcomes of Y and Z separately. Thus the information of X must be the sum of the informations of Y and Z; that is,

$$f(n) = f(n_1) + f(n_2)$$

where

$$n = n_1 n_2$$

This functional equation has many solutions. For example, $f(n)$ might be the logarithm of n_1, or $f(n)$ might be the number of factors into which n may be decomposed as a product of primes. However, there are other requirements of $f(n)$. The time required to transmit the outcome of experiment X will certainly be an increasing function of n. Hence, we need consider only those solutions of the functional equation that are increasing functions of n. The only such solutions turn out to be constant multiples of $\log n$; that is,

$$f(n) = c \log n$$

The simplest possible experiment we can imagine is one which has two equally likely outcomes, like flipping a coin. We use the information associated with such an experiment as the unit for measurement of information and call it *one bit*. When this unit has been defined, the information in an experiment with n equally likely outcomes is then precisely $\log_2 n$ bits.

Let us now test this definition of information and see if it does the things that we expect from it. For example, what is the information associated with an experiment whose outcome is certain? The experiment might be, for example, to see whether the sun will rise between midnight and noon tomorrow. There is only one outcome possible:

$$n = 1$$

The information associated with this experiment is

$$H = \log_2 1 = 0$$

When the outcome of the experiment is a foregone conclusion, the information carried by the conclusion is zero.

What is the information associated with an experiment which has eight equally likely outcomes? According to our formula, the information should be equal to*

$$\log 8 = 3$$

That is, it should have just three times as much information as that associated with flipping a coin. We can show that this is indeed the case by exhibiting the following code. Let the eight equally likely outcomes be identified as

$$HHH$$
$$HHT$$
$$HTH$$
$$THH$$
$$HTT$$
$$THT$$
$$TTH$$
$$TTT$$

* All logarithms are to the base 2 unless the contrary is specified.

The form of the code makes it obvious that the outcome of this experiment can be associated uniquely with the outcome of a succession of three coin-flipping experiments, and conversely. From the point of view of transmitting the information, it makes no difference whether the code word represents the outcome of three coin-flipping experiments or of one experiment with eight equally likely outcomes. Therefore, the information contained in one experiment with eight equally likely outcomes is three times that contained in an experiment like flipping a coin with two equally likely outcomes, that is,

$$H = \log 8 = 3 = \log 2 + \log 2 + \log 2$$

What happens if the various outcomes of the experiment are not equally likely? It is not immediately obvious that the definition of information can be extended. However, we can make a good try in the following way. Let us assume a situation (see Figure 1.4)

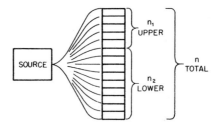

Figure 1.4   An idealized source with outputs of unequal probability.

where the experiment has n equally likely outcomes, grouped into two groups, an upper group of n_1 and a lower group of n_2, such that

$$n_1 + n_2 = n$$

Let us assume that we are not really interested in the particular message generated by the experiment, but only in whether the message is of the upper or of the lower group. We then have a situation where the significant output is one of two messages, having probabilities

$$p_1 = \frac{n_1}{n_1 + n_2}$$

for the upper message, and

$$p_2 = \frac{n_2}{n_1 + n_2}$$

for the lower, respectively. One way to find out how much information is associated with this is to start with the information associated with the n equally probable outcomes, and subtract the excess information with the n_1 or n_2 possible messages in the two subgroups. The information associated with one message among n equally likely messages, is

$$\log n$$

The information associated with one message among n_1 equally likely messages is

$$\log n_1$$

This occurs not all the time, however, but only for a proportion of the time equal to n_1/n. The information associated with one of n_2 equally likely messages is

$$\log n_2$$

and this occurs for a proportion of the time equal to n_2/n. Performing the arithmetic, we get

$$H = \log n - \frac{n_1}{n} \log n_1 - \frac{n_2}{n} \log n_2$$

$$= -p_1 \log p_1 - p_2 \log p_2$$

Since p_1 and p_2 are less than unity, their logarithms are negative. Thus, we can see that the information H is positive.

This argument suggests a form for the amount of information in a message generated by experiment X having n possible outcomes which are not all equally likely. Let the various outcomes have probabilities $p_1, p_2, \ldots, p_n$. In this case, the amount of information in the message generated by the experiment X is defined to be

$$H(x) = -p_1 \log p_1 - p_2 \log p_2 - \cdots - p_n \log p_n$$
$$= \sum_{i=1}^{n} -p_i \log p_i$$

This sum bears a formal resemblance to a quantity called entropy in statistical mechanics. For this reason $H(x)$ is also called the entropy function of $p_1, p_2, \ldots, p_n$.

Let us now look at this definition to see if we think it is appropriate as a measure of information. First of all, when the n outcomes are equally likely,

$$p_i = \frac{1}{n}$$
$$-\log p_i = \log n$$
$$\sum_{i=1}^{n} -p_i \log p_i = \sum_{i=1}^{n} \frac{1}{n} \log n$$
$$= \log n$$

as it should.

It will be shown in the next section that the information $H(x)$ generated by a discrete source with a fixed number of messages is a maximum if all the messages are equally probable. This fits our intuitive notion well: If all outcomes of the experiment are equally likely, the message must bear all the information we receive about the outcome; but if the outcomes are unequally likely, we have in advance something that a gambler, a stock speculator,

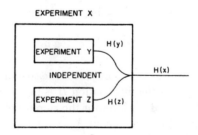

Figure 1.5   Illustrating the summing of information from two independent sources: $H(x) = H(y) + H(z)$.

or a weather forecaster would instantly recognize as information, and the additional information contributed by the message itself is less by that amount.

What if the experiment X consists of two independent experiments Y and Z? (See Figure 1.5.) Here the arithmetic is quite complicated, but ultimately we find

$$H(x) = H(y) + H(z)$$

In words, the information associated with X is the sum of information of its constituent experiments Y and Z. If Y and Z are not statistically independent* (see Figure 1.6), then

$$H(x) < H(y) + H(z)$$

This again is reasonable. Some of the $H(y)$ bits of information about the Y experiment give information about the possible outcome of the Z experiment and so are counted twice in the sum $H(y) + H(z)$. So far, the definition of information which we have come up with seems satisfactory.

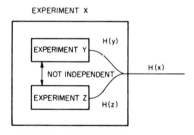

Figure 1.6   Illustrating the summing of information from two nonindependent sources: $H(x) < H(y) + H(z)$.

* Imagine the experiments Y and Z performed many times, and suppose that the results of the Y experiment are classified into sets according to the outcome of the Z experiment. Examine the probability distribution of the results of the Y experiment in each set: If the distribution does not vary from set to set, Y and Z are statistically independent. In plain but less precise language, the expected result of Y is the same whatever the result of Z.

1.4   Maximum Information from a Discrete Source

This tract originated with a set of lectures, during which it was often desirable to save time and energy by saying "it turns out that" or "it can be proved that," rather than to deal in detail with every point. Doubting Thomases could be reassured on the spot, by filling in any hiatus in the logic upon request.

This flexibility is lost in print: What is stated, is stated, and what is left out is left out, and there is no second chance. Nevertheless, the same economy is desirable. A good deal is still left out, but as evidence of good faith a point will be proved here to show the reader what he is missing.

It was stated earlier that the information generated by a discrete source with a fixed number n of outcomes is a maximum if the n outcomes are equally likely. How is this proved?

The public presentation of a proof usually begins with a statement of particular hypothesis and conditions, of unknown origin, and proceeds to the desired result as neatly as peeling a banana. But practitioners of the art, and amateurs who read the books of George Polya, realize that a proof is developed much differently: One assumes that all necessary requirements are met (what is "necessary" will be decided later) and forges ahead optimistically.

This is a *maximum* problem, so we try differential calculus. The quantity to be maximized is H, the variables p_i. They are related thus:

$$H = \sum_{i=1}^{n} - p_i \log p_i$$

There is an auxiliary condition on the variables:

$$\sum_{i=1}^{n} p_i = 1$$

This is tailor-made for the method of Lagrange's multipliers:

$$H - \lambda \sum p_i = \sum (\lambda - \log p_i) p_i$$

$$\frac{\partial}{\partial p_i} (H - \lambda \sum p_i) = \lambda - \log p_i - 1 = 0$$

$$\log p_i = -1 + \lambda \quad \text{for all } p_i$$

$$\begin{cases} p_i = \dfrac{1}{n} \quad \text{for all } p_i \\[2mm] H = \log n \end{cases}$$

So far, so good, but it is not yet a proof: We must show that the "solution" meets all the conditions of the problem, and that it is in fact a maximum.

One additional condition is

$$0 \le p_i \le 1 \qquad \text{for all } i$$

This, together with $\sum p_i = 1$, can be construed as defining a closed set consisting of a domain D including all points satisfying the first auxiliary condition for which $0 < p_i < 1$, together with its boundary. The condition is helpful: It allows us to invoke a general theorem that a bounded function on a closed set achieves its maximum and minimum. Can you show that H is bounded over this set? You will find it desirable to evaluate

$$\lim_{p \to 0} (-p \log p) = 0$$

and adopt the convention that, whenever any p_i takes the value 0, we replace the corresponding term in the sum by the limit.

We must also be wary of a maximum or a minimum on the boundary. You can show easily that if $p_i = 1$ for any i, the resulting value of H is not a maximum. Hence, at least two of the various p_i are different from 0, and none equal 1. Looking backward from a possible solution in which $p_i = 0$ for some i, you can throw out the terms for which this occurs and do the problem over with only those terms for which $p_i \ne 0$ at the maximum. The resulting H is less than that already formed. Thus points on the boundary are ruled out.

The function achieves its maximum, but not on the boundary. What else is needed to assure us that the unique point found by differentiation is the maximum? Some extra condition is required to guarantee that at the maximum, the function is sufficiently smooth: For the method based on differentiation to be valid, it suffices that at all points within the domain D the partial derivatives of H exist and are continuous. The outline of the proof is now complete.

The proof is really not yet complete. The big gap has been filled, but many little gaps remain. What passes for a proof at one time before one jury may be rejected at another time or by another audience. Our idea of what constitutes a valid proof is culturally conditioned, just like our idea of what constitutes virtue. But pursuit of this train of thought leads rapidly away from information theory.

The discovery that information is a maximum when the probabilities of the discrete outcomes are equal is misleading unless we know how sharp the maximum is. In fact, it is not very sharp. Figure 1.7 shows the information in a binary experiment as a func-

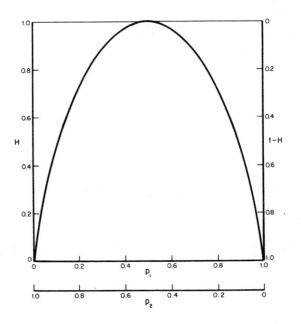

Figure 1.7   Information in one binary choice as a function of probability distribution: $H = -p_1 \log_2 p_1 - p_2 \log_2 p_2$.

tion of the probabilities p_1, p_2 of the two outcomes. The maximum information is 1 bit, achieved when $p_1 = p_2 = .5$. When the probabilities are .2, .8, the amount of information falls to .722 bit. When the probabilities are as unequal as .1, .9, the output falls just below half a bit; and for distribution .01, .99, the output is somewhat below one-tenth bit.

When there is a large number of choices, the situation is much the same. For example, suppose there are N outcomes with probabilities $p_k = k^{-\alpha} (\sum_1^N k^{-\alpha})^{-1}$; that is, the probability of occurrence of the kth most probable is proportional to $k^{-\alpha}$. Then the information $H = \sum_1^N -p_i \log p_i$ is precisely $\log_2 N$ for $\alpha = 0$. For large N, the information is asymptotically $\log_2 N$ for all α in the range $0 \le \alpha < 1$, and for $\alpha = 1$, $H \sim \frac{1}{2} \log_2 N$. The case $\alpha = 1$ corresponds fairly closely to the distribution of words in a single user's vocabulary, in which case it is sometimes called "Zipf's law."

Exercise for the Reader

Show that, for large N, if

$$p_k = k^{-\alpha} \left(\sum_{k=1}^N k^{-\alpha} \right)^{-1} \qquad 0 \le \alpha < 1$$

then

$$H = \sum_{k=1}^N -p_k \log p_k = \log N - \frac{\alpha}{1-\alpha} \log e + o(1)$$

Exercise for the Reader

Show that, for large N, if

$$p_k = k^{-1} \left(\sum_{k=1}^N k^{-1} \right)^{-1}$$

then

$$H = \sum_{k=1}^{N} - p_k \log p_k$$
$$= \tfrac{1}{2} \log N + \log \log N - \gamma \log_2 e + o(1)$$

where $\gamma = .5772 \cdots$ is Euler's constant.

1.5   Recapitulation

Let us recapitulate briefly. We started out with a model for a communication system that had an information source at one end and a destination at the other end. We have been looking for a definition of information that would be proportional to the time or the cost it takes to transmit the message from the message source to the destination. In order to get a firm hold on the problem, we successively restricted the information source until it was capable simply of putting forth n equally probable messages. In this case, we successfully defined information as $\log n$. We have generalized this definition slightly to the entropy function, which defines the amount of information generated by a message source capable of generating one of a finite set of n messages with known probability distribution. We have verified that this definition of information fulfills some elementary intuitive notions of how a measure of quantity of information ought to behave.

In a way, it does not seem that we have gone very far. The message source that we considered is extremely restricted, for it allows nothing more general than signals made up of discrete, uniquely distinguishable characters, such as teletypewriter messages. It does not include any message represented by a continuous waveform, such as the sound pressure of speech or the video signal which will generate a television picture. But surprisingly, the major hurdle in defining quantity of information has already been passed. In spite of the fact that speech waves and television video signals are continuous signals, in any real-life situation it is possible to distinguish only a finite number of tones or of picture intensities. The case of continuous messages can be reduced to the case of discrete messages already discussed, and the definition of quantity of information can be directly adapted to this use.

2

Applications to Discrete Channels

2.1   *Examples of Discrete Sources*

Let us now apply the definition of information which has just been stated to some discrete sources. Let us suppose that the experiment under consideration is that of shuffling a deck of 52 cards, and that the message is the particular order of the cards in the deck after shuffling. We shall define a *perfect shuffle* to mean that all of the possible orderings of the 52 cards are equally probable. Let us see how much information there is in a perfect shuffling experiment. The number of possible arrangements of the cards, according to well-known formulas in combinatorial analysis, is 52!* The amount of information associated with this experi-

---

* $n! = n(n - 1) \cdots 3 \cdot 2 \cdot 1$; e.g., $3! = 3 \cdot 2 \cdot 1 = 6, 4! = 4 \cdot 3 \cdot 2 \cdot 1 = 24$.

ment is

$$\log 52! = 225.7 \text{ bits}$$

Now let us look at another kind of shuffling experiment: Cut the deck into two packs, top (T) and bottom (B), at a random place, and then interleave T and B together. The interleaving operation consists of 52 steps, at each of which the bottom card of either T or B falls onto the top of the shuffled deck. The shuffle is completely described by a sequence of 52 letters T or B. (The ith letter is T if at the ith step the card fell from the bottom of packet T.) The position of the cut may be found from the sequence by counting the number of T's. There are only 2^{52} possible sequences of T and B, and hence only 2^{52} possible outcomes of the shuffling experiment. Even if we suppose all these outcomes to be equally probable, the maximum amount of information associated with this shuffling experiment is log of 2^{52}, or 52 bits.

Exercise

How many times do you have to cut and interleave a deck in order to achieve something approximating a perfect shuffle? We learned earlier that the information associated with a sequence of independent experiments is not greater than the sum of the informations developed by the experiments independently. Each cut and interleave shuffling operation generates at most 52 bits of information. A perfect shuffle generates 225.7 bits of information. Therefore, no sequence of fewer than 5 cutting and interleaving shuffles could possibly generate a perfect shuffle. We can say with confidence that to shuffle a deck fairly by cutting and interleaving, you must repeat the operation at least 5 times. There is no guarantee, of course, that this will produce a perfect shuffling operation: All we have found out is that if you cut and interleave fewer than 5 times, it certainly will not produce a perfect shuffle.

As another example, let us consider the information content of ordinary written English. To simplify the problems, let us talk about "telegraph English," which has no punctuation, no paragraphs, no lower case letters, and so forth. In this case, we have 27 symbols, the letters *a* to *z* and a space.

To get an upper limit to the amount of information, we can simply assume that all 27 symbols are equally probable. This sets an upper limit to the amount of information of $\log 27 = 4.76$ bits per letter.

This estimate is certainly pessimistic, because we know that the letters are not equally probable. By carrying out a count of letters in a sufficiently large sample of text, we can get an idea of the relative probabilities of spaces and letters in English text. Using these data, we can apply the formula we have developed to find out that the information in English text is not more than about 4 bits per letter.

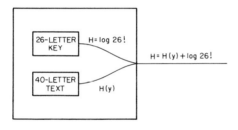

Figure 2.1   Information in a 40-letter text coded with a simple substitution code.

This estimate can be refined somewhat with observations taken from cryptography. Consider the construction of a substitution cryptogram. In such a cryptogram, for each letter in the alphabet some other letter is substituted. The table which tells which letter is substituted for which is called the key, and it is not hard to find that the number of possible keys is 26!. If we view the cryptogram (see Figure 2.1) as a compound experiment X whose two parts are Y, the communication of the clear text, and Z, the choice of a key from one of 26! possibilities, the total information associated with this compound experiment is no greater than

$H(y) + \log 26!$ bits. We understand that substitution cryptograms of 40 letters can usually be solved, that is, given a 40-letter cryptogram, the information in both the text and the key can be recovered. Since 40 letters can contain no more than 40 log 27 bits of information, one concludes that

$$40 \log 27 \geq H(y) + \log 26!$$

and hence that the information in a 40-letter English message is

$$H(y) \leq 40 \log 27 - \log 26! \sim 100$$

The information in an English message is consequently no greater than 2.5 bits per letter.

By using more and more refined arguments, it has been shown* that the information content of ordinary English text is about 1 bit per letter.

Exercise

A Problem Solved with Information Theory

You are given a balance and 9 coins. Eight of the coins are equal in weight, but the ninth is defective, and weighs somewhat more or less than each of the other 8.

Problem: Devise a way to determine, in 3 weighings, which is the odd coin, and whether it is lighter or heavier than the others.

It appears that we can put equal numbers of coins in the 2 pans of the balance, upon which it will tip to the left, balance, or tip to the right. The most information you can get per weighing is

$$\log_2 3 = 1.58 \text{ bits}$$

In 3 weighings, not more than 4.74 bits can be generated. Assuming complete ignorance of the identity of the odd coin, and whether it is light or heavy, you see that you are asked to identify one of 18 equally likely possibilities. This requires

* C. E. Shannon, "Prediction and Entropy of Printed English," *Bell System Tech. J.*, *30*, 50–64 (January, 1951).

$$\log_2 18 = 4.16 \text{ bits} < 4.74 \text{ bits}$$

So far, there is no conflict.

There are, however, a great many ways to put the coins on the balance, and we can use information theory to devise a strategy. For a first attempt, try the following:

Strategy: At each weighing, generate the maximum possible amount of information.

But how much information is gained in 1 weighing? Let

p_l = probability that balance tips left
p_b = probability that balance does not tip
p_r = probability that balance tips right

Then the information generated in one weighing is

$$H = -p_l \log p_l - p_b \log p_b - p_r \log p_r$$

We know this is a maximum if the probabilities are all equal. Hence, the strategy leads to a simpler statement: If possible, weigh so that tipping to the left, balancing, and tipping to the right are equally probable.

Suppose we put n coins in the left pan, n in the right, and $9 - 2n$ are not weighed. Then

$$P_b = \frac{(9 - 2n)}{9}$$
$$p_l = p_r = \frac{n}{9}$$

For all of them to be equal, n must be 3.

Hence the first step: Three coins (say 1, 2, and 3) in the left pan; 3 (say 4, 5, and 6) in the right pan, and 3 (say 7, 8, and 9) left unweighed.

What is the second step? We must distinguish 2 cases: The balance does or does not balance in the first step.

If the balance does balance in the first step, the defective coin is 7, 8, or 9. We can throw away 1 to 6, and repeat the same reasoning to find a desirable attempt: Weigh 1 coin in each pan, and have 1 unweighed. The reader can verify that this leads to a solution.

But suppose the balance tilts in step 1. What then? In order to achieve a probability $\frac{1}{3}$ that it will balance in step 2, it is easy to see that only 4 of the 6 coins 1 to 6 can be in step 2. But to have equal probability that the balance will tip left or right is harder: We must, with probability $\frac{1}{2}$, shift the odd coin to the other pan. These conditions are satisfied, for example, by

Removing coins 1 and 4
Interchanging coins 2 and 5
Leaving coins 3 and 6

It is easy to see that if the result of step 2 is an even balance, then 1 or 4 is odd; if the sense of imbalance is different from step 1, then 2 or 5 is odd; and if the sense of imbalance is the same as in step 1, then 3 or 6 is odd. The third weighing tells which is odd, and whether it is heavy or light.

Thus the strategy is completely successful.

You will note that the full potential of the third step is not used, suggesting that more information could be drawn from 3 weighings. Perhaps you could start with 10 or 11 coins and still tell which is odd and whether it is light or heavy. On the other hand, no sequence of 3 steps each leading to an even balance can ever tell whether the odd coin is lighter or heavier. As you can see, the problem of determining the largest number of coins from which you can sort and classify 1 odd coin in 3 weighings is rather subtle.

Exercise for the Reader

Given 27 coins, 26 of equal weight and 1 heavier than the rest. Devise a strategy to identify the heavy coin in 3 weighings. Can you solve the analogous problem with more than 27 coins?

2.2   Coding for Noiseless Channels

It is useful here to introduce the idea of an *encoder*. An encoder may be described as a purely deterministic device which converts a message in one set of symbols into a new message, usually in a different set of symbols. For example, a handwritten English message may be converted into a pattern of holes punched on a tape, then into a sequence of electrical impulses on a teletype wire, back into English letters by a teletypewriter, and finally translated from English into French. The first three of these four operations are reversible encodings. That means that each incoming message can be encoded in only one way, and conversely, that no two different incoming messages are ever encoded alike. Translation from English into French, however, is not usually an encoding, because it involves random choices. For example, the English word "robbery" may be translated into either "vol" or "brigandage." Even assuming that all such choices were settled in advance, one would undoubtedly find some French words representing several English ones, for example, "vol" for both "robbery" and "theft." Then the encoding would not be reversible.

A *reversible encoder* transforms messages into encoded messages in a one-to-one way; one gets the same amount of information from the encoded message as from the original message. One would like to conclude that a reversible encoder driven by an information source is a new information source which generates information at the same rate as the driving source. However, this conclusion requires further assumptions about the encoder. For example, the encoder might just store the incoming message, and re-emit it at a slower rate. Such an encoder would ultimately require an unlimited amount of storage space. However, if a reversible encoder has only a finite number of internal states (for example, if it is made from a finite number of relays or magnetic cores or switching tubes with a finite memory), then the encoder output has the same information rate as its input.

We also need to talk about an idealized noiseless *channel* for transmission of discrete messages. An ideal channel has a finite list of symbols which it can transmit without error. A certain time is required to transmit each symbol. The times required to transmit the various symbols may not be the same.

The combination of a channel fed by a source may be regarded as a new source which generates the message at the receiving end (see Figure 2.2). The information rate of the received message will depend on the transmitting source. For example, suppose a channel can transmit English letters and word spaces at the rate of 1 symbol per second. When the channel transmits English text, it has a rate, as we have seen before, of about 1 bit per second. If the same channel is connected to a source which produces letters and spaces independently, with probability 1/27 for each kind of symbol, the rate is $\log 27 = 4.76$ bits per second. The largest rate at which one can signal over a channel, for all choices of the source, is called the capacity of the channel. The capacity of the English letter channel just discussed is 4.76 bits per second.

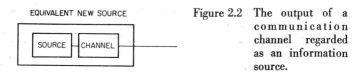

EQUIVALENT NEW SOURCE

| SOURCE | CHANNEL |

Figure 2.2 The output of a communication channel regarded as an information source.

In the example of the English text source connected to the English letter channel, one feels that much of the capability of the channel is wasted. With an English text source as input, the channel transmits information at a rate much lower than that attainable with other sources.

Is it possible to speed up the source and still use the same channel? The answer is yes, and an encoder provides the means for doing so. It is possible to encode English text reversibly in such a way that the encoded messages use fewer letters than the original messages. Then the encoded text may be transmitted at a higher information rate than the original text could.

In general, if we say that a channel has a capacity of C bits per second, we mean that the output of any source of information rate less than C bits per second may be transmitted over the channel by placing a suitable reversible encoder between the source and the channel. No reversible encoder will transform the output of any source having an information rate greater than C so that it can be transmitted through the channel without error.

To illustrate how the encoding process works, consider a very simple example. The source has two symbols: *A*, with probability $\frac{4}{5}$; and *B*, with probability $\frac{1}{5}$. Successive symbols are generated independently, at a rate of 80 per minute (see Figure 2.3).

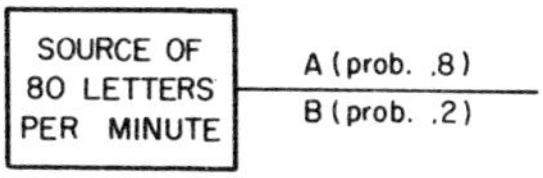

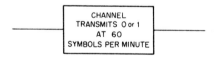

Figure 2.3   An information source.

The information rate of this source is

$$H = -.2 \log .2 - .8 \log .8$$

$$= .72 \text{ bit per letter}$$

$$\frac{H}{T} = .72 \frac{80}{60}$$

$$= .96 \text{ bit per second}$$

So much for the source: now for the channel. The channel (see Figure 2.4) transmits two symbols, zero and one, without constraint, and requires precisely 1 second of transmission time to transmit either symbol. The channel capacity is thus 1 bit per second.

CHANNEL
TRANSMITS 0 or 1
AT 60
SYMBOLS PER MINUTE

Figure 2.4   A communication channel. (Will the information from the source of Figure 2.3 pass through the channel?)

The simplest encoder we can imagine is the one shown in the following table:

Letters	Probability	Digits	Weighted number of digits
A	.8	0	.8
B	.2	1	.2
			1.0

The total weighted number of digits is

1.0 digit per letter = 80 digits per minute

An example of a stream of letters and their encoding digits is

A B A A A A B A A A A A B A B A A A A A A A A A B A B A A A A
0 1 0 0 0 0 1 0 0 0 0 0 1 0 1 0 0 0 0 0 0 0 0 0 1 0 1 0 0 0 0

With such an encoder, 80 digits per minute are generated, and the channel will not tolerate them. A better encoder is shown in the next table.

Letters	Probability	Digits	Weighted number of digits
AA	.64	0	.64
AB	.16	10	.32
BA	.16	110	.48
BB	.04	111	.12
			1.56

Here, instead of encoding 1 message letter at a time, we group the message in bunches of 2 letters, and encode the 2 letters together. The relative probabilities of various groups of 2 letters vary over quite a range, as indicated in the second column. In order to gain efficiency in the coding, we use a short group of digits for a more common letter group, and reserve longer groups of digits for the less common letter groups. The last column, weighted number of digits, is the probability of a given digit group multiplied by the number of digits in the group. Summing the last column over all letter groups, one finds an average digit-group length of 1.56 digits for 2 letters, or .78 digit per letter. The encoder turns out 62.4 digits per minute, still more than the channel will take. The same stream of letters is now encoded thus:

A B A A A A B A A A A A B A B A A A A A A A A B A B A A A A
10 0   0 110 0   0 110 110 0   0   0 10 10   0   0

The 30 letters are now encoded in 24 digits, 9 one's and 15 zero's.
The reader can verify that if the digits are run together without
spaces, they can still be separated unambiguously into symbols
from our finite alphabet. Such a code is called *segmented*.

We can carry this a bit further, as shown in the next table.

Letters	Probability	Digits	Weighted number of digits
AAA	.512	0	.512
AAB	.128	100	.384
ABA	.128	101	.384
BAA	.128	110	.384
ABB	.032	11100	.160
BAB	.032	11101	.160
BBA	.032	11110	.160
BBB	.008	11111	.040
			2.184

In this example, each group of 3 letters is encoded in a single
digit group. The more common letter groups are encoded in short
digit groups, and the less common groups in longer digit groups.
Doing the arithmetic exactly as before, we find that the average
digit-group length for three letters is 2.184 digits. This results in
an average of .728 digit per letter, and the encoder produces 58.24
digits per minute, which can be transmitted by the channel. We
already know that the information content of this source is .72
bit per letter, and therefore, no reversible encoder could encode
it in less than .72 digit per letter on the average. The encoder
illustrated is only about 1 per cent less efficient than the ideal.
The stream of letters given before is now encoded thus:

A B A A A A B A A A A A B A B A A A A A A A A B A B A A A A
101   0   110   0 11101   0   0   100   101   0

The stream of 30 letters is now encoded in 22 digits, 11 ones
and 11 zeros. The fact that the number of ones and zeros grow

closer and closer together is not an accident. We know that the maximum capacity of a 2-symbol source is reached only when the two symbols have equal probability. Our encoder must bow to this fact if it is to use the channel efficiently.

This encoder must have some storage capacity, and must introduce some delay. For example, 3 incoming letters must arrive and be stored before the outgoing digit group is identified. Furthermore, the long digit groups are transmitted more slowly than the incoming 3-letter groups are generated; and signals must be stored until a string of AAA's allows the encoder and transmission channel to catch up. In this simple example, no finite storage capacity will guarantee flawless performance, but the probability of exceeding a storage requirement of a few hundred symbols is extremely small.

The above example illustrates the general coding theorem, which can be loosely expressed as follows: Given a channel and a message source that generates information at a rate less than the channel capacity, it is possible to devise an encoder which will allow the output of the message source, suitably encoded, to be transmitted through the channel.

Exercise

How to Win at "20 Questions"

In a popular parlor game called "20 Questions," one person who is "it" mentally identifies something, usually a material object or a living being, knowledge of which is available to the other participants. The others try to make a unique identification by asking questions answerable by "yes" or "no" which are answered truthfully. They are allowed a maximum of 20 such questions. In one form of the game, they are allowed 3 additional questions of the form "is it . . .?" (naming a particular tentative unique identification). If an answer to such a question is "yes," the asker wins; otherwise, the one who is "it" wins. The winner is "it" for the next round.

The amount of information available in the replies to 23

yes–no questions is no more than 23 bits. Experience shows that the game is proportioned so that one of the askers usually wins, not the one who is "it." This reflects on the sparseness of human imagination. The language has several hundred thousand words; a large library has several million books; there are several hundred million people living in the United States. A truly random choice from one of these classes would require at least 19, 22, or 27 bits, respectively, to identify. With the additional questions required to identify the particular class, the total probably exceeds 23, and the one who is "it" could win the game with high probability.

A simpler way for the ambitious contestant to win is to pick a large number — say 8 digits or more. Of course, it is uninspiring for the others to hear, after 23 fruitless questions, "I was thinking of 55,880,402," or even "I was thinking of the 17th name in the second column of the forty-first page of the telephone directory of the seventh largest city in Indiana." If you use such a strategy, you will win with high probability, but your adversaries will find it dull and probably will criticize you for spoiling the game. Your decision about whether to adopt this strategy depends on how great a price you are willing to pay to win.

3

Channel Capacity

3.1 Channel Capacity of an Analog Channel *

In the coding theorem stated in the previous section, we have
implicitly defined the channel capacity of a channel: If a channel
can transmit C binary digits per second (but no more), its channel
capacity is C. It is easy to apply this definition to a channel which
transmits strings of zeros and ones at a fixed rate, as in the previous example. It is equally easy to apply it to a teletypewriter
transmission channel which transmits sequences of letters and
spaces at a rate fixed by the terminal equipment. But this is not

---

* This chapter attempts to explain in simple terms some of the important
results of "Communication in the Presence of Noise," by C. E. Shannon,
Proc. IRE, *47*, 10–21 (1959).

really very useful, because there has never been very much doubt about the capacity of such a channel. Suppose we have a more general channel: How do we determine its channel capacity?

This question really hinges on a determination of how many distinguishable signals the channel can transmit. To answer this question, we would like to have a way of identifying individual signals and distinguishing them one from another. What we really need is a catalog of signals.

Let us take as an example a channel capable of transmitting continuous waves with a finite bandwidth, free of distortion, but with uniform Gaussian noise of known power. Let us now identify and catalog the signals which can be transmitted through this channel.

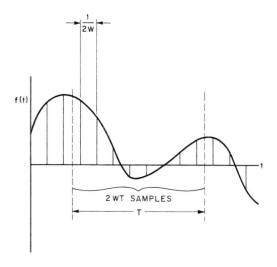

Figure 3.1   Sampling of a band-limited function of bandwidth W.

We can get immediate help from the sampling theorem, a purely mathematical theorem now well-known in the communication art, which will be stated here without proof (see Figure 3.1).

If a function of time $f(t)$ contains no frequencies higher than W cycles per second, the function is uniquely determined by giving its ordinates at a series of points spaced $1/(2W)$ seconds apart.

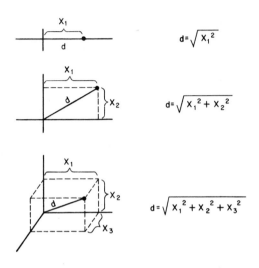

Figure 3.2   Multidimensional geometry.

If we now let W be the bandwidth of the communication channel in question, we can identify any signal which the channel can transmit with a sequence of ordinates spaced $1/(2W)$ seconds apart. If we take a piece of this signal lasting only a finite time, say T, then the number of ordinates falling in this time range is $2TW$.

We can now introduce some geometrical ideas to help us along with the cataloging process (Figure 3.2). A quantity which is identified by one number can be represented as a point on the straight line. A quantity identified by two numbers can be represented by a point on a plane: This is the familiar procedure used to plot graphs. A quantity identified by three numbers can be represented by a point in three-dimensional space. Similarly, our signal identified by $2TW$ numbers can be identified with a point in a (necessarily imaginary) geometrical space of $2TW$ dimensions. We imagine the $2TW$ identifying numbers to be the coordinates of a point, measured along $2TW$ mutually perpendicular axes.

If we compute energy E in the signal, we find, except for a scale factor,* that

$$E = \frac{1}{2W} \sum x_n{}^2$$

where x_n is the nth coordinate, that is, the nth sample of $f(t)$. If we compute the distance from the origin to a point in the space which represents the same signal, we find

$$d = \sqrt{\sum x_n{}^2}$$

Thus

$$d^2 = 2WE$$
$$= 2WTP$$

where P is the signal power. In other words, in this geometric visualization of continuous signals, geometrical distance is proportional to the square root of the power. The distance between two points in space is proportional to the square root of the power of the difference of the two signals which the points represent. Signals of power less than P all lie within the sphere of radius $d = \sqrt{2WTP}$.

Now let us consider what happens to a signal as it goes through our channel. In Figure 3.3, we follow the geometric analogy, but represent the space of $2WT$ dimensions as two-dimensional space. A given input signal or output signal is represented by a point in the space. The distance between two points is proportional to the square root of the power of the difference of the two signals. Assume that the signal power is P and that the power added by the noise in the channel is N. Assume that we know the position of the point in space representing the signal before it is transmitted

* If the signal is electrical and $f(t)$ is the instantaneous amplitude in volts, the scale factor is the real part of the circuit admittance in mhos. All sums are over the range $(1,2TW)$, unless otherwise stated.

SPACE OF 2WT DIMENSIONS

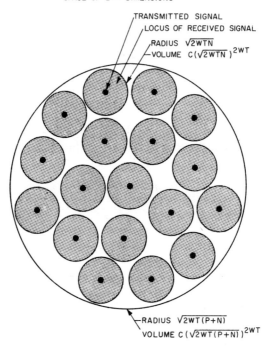

Figure 3.3   Transmitted and received signals in $2WT$-dimensional
signal space.

through the channel. Where is this point at the output end of
the channel? We do not know exactly, but we know approximately: It is somewhere in a sphere of radius $\sqrt{2WTN}$ centered
around the point representing the transmitted signal. In the figure,
this sphere is represented by a stippled circle. Just as the area of
a circle is proportional to the square of its radius, and the volume
of the sphere is proportional to the cube of its radius, so the
volume of this hypersphere is proportional to the $2WT$ power of
its radius, say,

$$V = K(\sqrt{2WTN})^{2WT}$$

where K is a constant whose numerical value is not important here.

The output of this channel consists of a signal plus noise, and has power approximately $P + N$. If we consider the whole family of possible outputs, they lie in a sphere of radius $\sqrt{2WT(P + N)}$. In the figure, this is represented by the large circle. The volume of this hypersphere is

$$V = K(\sqrt{2WT(P + N)})^{2WT}$$

where K is the same unspecified constant as before. Now let us assume that we have a number M of transmitted signals such that the regions of uncertainty associated with them when they are perturbed by the noise are nonoverlapping. Then the large hypersphere contains M nonoverlapping small hyperspheres. The volume of the large hypersphere is at least M times the volume of one of the small hyperspheres. If we write down this inequality and solve for M we get

$$K(\sqrt{2WT(P + N)})^{2WT} \geq MK(\sqrt{2WTN})^{2WT}$$
$$M \leq \left(\sqrt{\frac{N + P}{N}}\right)^{2WT} = \left(1 + \frac{P}{N}\right)^{TW}$$

The ratio P/N is the familiar signal-to-noise ratio. We can find the average rate of information transfer thus:

$$\log M \leq TW \log\left(1 + \frac{P}{N}\right)$$
$$\frac{1}{T}\log M \leq W \log\left(1 + \frac{P}{N}\right)$$

This gives us an upper limit for the channel capacity of this channel.

To get a more useful result, we also need a lower limit. In fact, the lower limit turns out to be the same as the upper limit: We have an equality instead of an inequality. The details of the mathematical development are rather complex, and it is unnecessary to work them out here. However, we shall sketch the idea behind the proof, because it yields some important results.

The idea is as follows. We fix a certain number M of points in this space as signals, without regard for spacing to avoid overlapping regions. A particular selection of M points constitutes a particular code for transmitting signals. After having picked M particular points, we compute the probability of error at the receiving end. This is the probability that a point in the space (observed at the receiving end of the channel) which is close to one code point is also close enough to another point so that it might be wrongly identified. The probability of error is then averaged over all possible choices of codes. After going through all the arithmetic, geometry, and trigonometry, we obtain the following result:

$$\frac{1}{T} \log M \geq W \log\left(1 + \frac{P}{N}\right) + \frac{1}{T} \log E_{av}$$

where E_{av} is the averaged probability of error. (Note that $E_{av} < 1$, so that $\log E_{av}$ is negative.)

We need to observe two things about this inequality. First, for some code choices, the error rate must be at least as low as the average error rate. Second, if we make T sufficiently large, we can make $(1/T) \log E_{av}$ as small as desired, and hence we can make

$$\frac{1}{T} \log M$$

as close as we wish to

$$W \log\left(1 + \frac{P}{N}\right)$$

and still make the average error rate as small as we please. Another way of saying this is

$$\text{lub}\left\{\frac{1}{T} \log M\right\} = W \log\left(1 + \frac{P}{N}\right)$$

(where lub signifies least upper bound) for any value of average error rate, no matter how small.

We define this bound as the channel capacity, and can assert with confidence that there exist codes which permit transmission at a rate as close as desired to the channel capacity,

$$C = W \log \left(1 + \frac{P}{N}\right)$$

with an arbitrarily small error rate.

The discussion is not complete without a study of what kind of codes are required for signaling at a rate acceptably close to the limit. It is obvious at once that efficient coding requires a code whose elements, as represented by points in the signal space of $2TW$ dimensions, are fairly uniformly distributed. This is true because nonuniform distribution of the points would make gaps and holes in the signal-space representation into which further useful code elements could be placed.

Furthermore, any coding that allows transmission at a rate near the channel capacity is subject to a sudden large increase in error rate if the noise increases slightly. This is sometimes called a threshold effect. The threshold effect arises because an increase in noise reduces the channel capacity. When the actual channel capacity is reduced below the signaling rate, the information output of the channel is limited to at most the channel capacity by the introduction of errors. As an example, let us assume a channel with a bandwidth W of 10^6 cycles per second and a signal-to-noise ratio P/N of unity. Then the channel capacity is

$$C = W \log \left(1 + \frac{P}{N}\right) = 10^6 \text{ bits per second}$$

Suppose we have a code allowing signaling at a rate $.8C$, that is,

$$R = 8 \times 10^5 \text{ bits per second,}$$

with a very small error rate.

Now suppose the noise increases 3 decibels, so that the signal-to-noise ratio is .5. The new channel capacity is

$$C = 10^6 \log (1 + .5) = 5.85 \times 10^5$$

which is less than the signaling rate. To reduce the actual information content of the output from 8×10^5 to 5.85×10^5 bits per second in an ideal binary symmetric channel like that discussed in the next section would require an error rate of .045. Any practical equipment would make errors at a higher rate. Such an error rate makes the equipment virtually useless for any digital transmission such as teletype or data transmission. The only remedy is to recode the input to transmit at a lower rate.

Finally, to achieve transmission at a rate approaching the channel capacity requires a very large number M of distinct elements in the code. A general formula for the relation of code-group size and error rate is hard to develop, but bounds can be calculated which show that the error rate decreases exponentially with an exponent which is roughly proportional both to the number of bits carried by one code element and to the ratio of channel capacity C to signaling rate R. As a particular example, which is typical of the general situation, Fano* has chosen a code consisting of M distinct orthogonal waveforms each having the same total energy. He shows that

$$P(e) = K2^{-\nu\alpha C/R}$$

where

$P(e)$ is the probability of error

K is a function of the order of unity

ν is the number of binary digits constituting a message

or

$2^\nu = M$ is the number of distinct messages in the alphabet

C is the channel capacity

R is the actual signaling rate

and

α is a particular function of R and C of the following form

$$\alpha = \alpha\left(\frac{R}{C}\right) = \frac{1}{2} - \frac{R}{C} \qquad 0 \le \frac{R}{C} \le \frac{1}{4}$$

$$= \left[1 - \sqrt{\frac{R}{C}}\right]^2 \qquad \frac{1}{4} \le \frac{R}{C} \le 1$$

The function $\alpha C/R$ as a function of C/R is plotted in Figure 3.4. For values of C/R greater than 4, $\alpha C/R = -1 + C/2R$.

For example, to achieve an error rate $P(e) = 10^{-5}$ with a sig-

* Reference 1 in the Bibliography, pages 205 ff.

naling rate 95 per cent of the capacity, that is, $R/C = 0.95$, requires about 25,000 bits per message element, or about $M = 10^{7,500}$ distinct code elements. For a signaling rate 50 per cent of the channel capacity, about 100 bits per message element, or 10^{30} distinct code elements are required. For signaling at 25 per cent of capacity, 17 bits or about 100,000 distinct code elements are required. This is beginning to be reasonable, but the channel is not used at anything close to its ideal capacity.

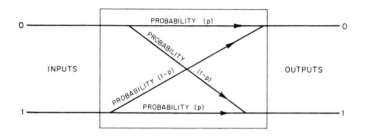

Figure 3.4   A binary symmetric channel.

The choice of signal elements in Fano's particular example form a symmetric configuration in signal space, but are not symmetric about the origin. The simple step of modifying each of the elements by subtracting from it the average of all the elements of the set produces another related set of code elements for which the analogous error estimate is

$$P(e) = K2^{-\nu\alpha(1-2^{-\nu})C/R}$$

The distinction is of almost no interest except for small values of ν; it is mentioned here only because a practical instance corresponding to a value $\nu = 1$ will be described later.

3.2   *Channel Capacity of Discrete Channels*

It was observed in Chapter 2 that the capacity of a noiseless discrete channel is quite obvious. But no real channel is ever noiseless: If it were, we would attempt to lower the power or increase the signaling rate, or do something else to lower the cost and increase the efficiency, until some evidence of errors made itself felt.

Transmission over noisy discrete channels is of practical interest, and it is worthwhile to know what the channel capacity of a noisy discrete channel is, and what code to use to transmit at a rate approaching the channel capacity.

The use of the word *noise* with respect to a discrete channel is a conceit of the information theorist: He does not mean ripples, distortion, or minor imperfections in a waveform, but only disturbances which cause the output to be wrongly interpreted, or, in simpler terms, errors.

The simplest discrete channel is a binary symmetric channel (Figure 3.4). This channel accepts 2 code symbols, say 0 and 1, at some rate, and puts forth the same 2 symbols at the same rate; however, it makes mistakes, randomly distributed, with probability p independent of the incoming stream of symbols.

What is the channel capacity of such a channel? We can guess the capacity with the following argument: Suppose we add to the channel a fictitious "error compensator" which produces, at the same rate as the channel, a stream of E's and C's, and E every time the channel makes an error and a C when the channel is correct. Such a device could be regarded as an information source, and as such has a rate

$$H_{ec} = -p \log p - (1 - p) \log (1 - p) \text{ bits per symbol}$$

In conjunction with the channel it can be used to produce an error-free output having an information content of 1 bit per symbol. If we agree that the information in the error compensator is "used up" in correcting the errors, then we can deduce that the channel capacity of the channel is

$$H_c = 1 - H_{ec}$$
$$= 1 + p \log p + (1 - p) \log (1 - p) \text{ bits per symbol}$$

This derivation is not rigorous, but the answer is right. The right way to go about proving the result is similar to the method used in the last section for analog channels: Assume an arbitrary diversity of codings and find a lower limit (and an upper limit) for the error rate. In Reference 1 of the Bibliography it is proved that codes exist which permit transmission through a binary symmetric channel with arbitrarily low error rate at a signaling rate as close as desired to H_c bits per symbol, and that no code (or at least none of a class which seems to be sufficiently general) can lead to signaling through this channel at a higher rate without a finite and irreducible error rate.

Figure 1.7 can be used as a plot of $H_c = 1 - H_{ec}$ as a function of p. Use the scale for $1 - H$ on the right, and let either p_1 or p_2 equal p.

At first sight it seems implausible that any code can reduce the error rate below p. A simple example from a class of codes called "parity-check codes" will show how this is done. Let the sixteen 7-digit code symbols be

$$
\begin{matrix}
0 & 0 & 0 & 0 & 0 & 0 & 0 \\
1 & 1 & 0 & 1 & 0 & 0 & 1 \\
0 & 1 & 0 & 1 & 0 & 1 & 0 \\
1 & 0 & 0 & 0 & 0 & 1 & 1 \\
1 & 0 & 0 & 1 & 1 & 0 & 0 \\
0 & 1 & 0 & 0 & 1 & 0 & 1 \\
1 & 1 & 0 & 0 & 1 & 1 & 0 \\
0 & 0 & 0 & 1 & 1 & 1 & 1 \\
1 & 1 & 1 & 0 & 0 & 0 & 0 \\
0 & 0 & 1 & 1 & 0 & 0 & 1 \\
1 & 0 & 1 & 1 & 0 & 1 & 0 \\
0 & 1 & 1 & 0 & 0 & 1 & 1 \\
0 & 1 & 1 & 1 & 1 & 0 & 0 \\
1 & 0 & 1 & 0 & 1 & 0 & 1 \\
0 & 0 & 1 & 0 & 1 & 1 & 0 \\
1 & 1 & 1 & 1 & 1 & 1 & 1 \\
\end{matrix}
$$

It will be observed that the digits are chosen so that

the sum of the 1st, 3rd, 5th, and 7th digits is even,
the sum of the 2nd, 3rd, 6th, and 7th digits is even, and
the sum of the 4th, 5th, 6th, and 7th digits is even.

These 3 sums check are checks of oddness and evenness, and are called *parity checks*: Thus this class of codes gets its name. If any single digit in such a code group is erroneously transmitted, a new code group is generated which will not satisfy the parity checks, and thus the presence of an error is announced. However, this particular code is also self-correcting: the procedure is this. If the first parity check fails, write 1; if the second fails, write 2; and if the third check fails, write 4; then add. The sum is the position of the erroneous digit. For example, suppose 0 1 0 1 1 1 0 is received. The 3 parity checks fail, succeed, and fail, respectively, so we write $1 + 4 = 5$, showing that the fifth digit is wrong, and that the correct block is 0 1 0 1 0 1 0, one of the members of the code set. If you want to know how this particular code works, you can read a fuller description by Hamming*; Reference 1 of the Bibliography gives a general and systematic treatment to the parity checking and other types of error-correcting codes.

Exercise

The Arithmetic of a Simple Parity Check

The numbers 0, 1, 2, 3, 4, 5, 6, 7, can be written in binary notation 0, 1, 10, 11, 100, 101, 110, 111. In literal notation, n is represented by $a_2 a_1 a_0$, where $a = 0$ or 1, and

$$n = a_2 \cdot 2^2 + a_1 \cdot 2^1 + a_0 \cdot 2^0$$

For the parity-check system described above, digits are chosen for the three parity checks according to the binary representation of their numerical position (first, second, third, etc., digit). The several checks include all those positions for which $a_0 = 1$, or $a_1 = 1$, or $a_2 = 1$, respectively. Satisfy yourself that you know how and why this check works. Demonstrate your mastery by devising a check for a 15-digit code block according to the same principle.

The particular parity-check code described above is useful only for correcting single errors. If there are 2 or more errors in a

---

* R. W. Hamming, "Error Detecting and Error Correcting Codes," *Bell System Tech. J.*, 29, 147–160 (April, 1950).

group, it will be decoded wrong, with a resultant loss of 4 bits of information. Such a code is only useful for improving a channel whose error rate is already very low. For example, if the error rate of the channel is 10^{-5} per symbol, this code will permit transmission at a reduced rate with an error rate of less than 10^{-11}; but if the error rate of the channel is .01, application of this code reduces the error rate only to .0085 per bit. The reason is that single errors are corrected only at the expense of allowing double errors to spoil a whole group of 7.

Error-correcting codes which work in noisier channels can also be developed, but they are complex and therefore the code groups are longer and more numerous. Mathematical estimates of the error rate achievable with codes of a given length can be made, but they are more complex than the particular estimate cited before for analog channels, because they depend not only on the ratio of the signaling speed of to the channel capacity, but also on the noise probability of the channel itself. But it is still true that the error rate achievable decreases exponentially with the code-group length. An elegant geometric construction for an estimate of the exponent is found in Figures 7.3 and 7.4 of Reference 1 of the Bibliography.

The practical consequence of such estimates is that we would like to use codes with code groups having 100 digits or so. Generating such a code is not difficult, but decoding it is made very complex by the fact that the decoder must be prepared to deal with 2^{100}, or roughly 10^{30}, different possible code groups. It is not presently practical to design decoders to perform the computations necessary to handle such a large number of possible inputs.

An escape from this dilemma is provided by sequential coding (Reference 10 of the Bibliography). In a sequential code, the code digits are not generated or decoded in blocks, but one at a time. Each code digit is based jointly on the incoming information to be coded and on the details of the code digits already encoded. In the decoding process, only two choices are available for a single digit: Either it is right, or the channel produced an error and the digit it delivered is wrong. The decoder acts on the optimistic assumption that the channel is correct, but reserves the option

to change its mind. If a sequence of digits comes out of the channel which is inconsistent with the known structure of the code,
the decoder goes back a few spaces and assumes 1, or 2, or the
minimum number of recent errors which "makes sense." This is
similar to what a human being does when listening to speech:
He recognizes syllables and words, but if they don't hang together,
he goes back in his mind and alters a few here and there so that
the speech makes sense. A sequential coder and decoder has been
built which is capable of transmitting with an error rate of less
than 10^{-6} through a binary symmetric channel with an error rate
of .07 at the cost of a reduction of speed to one-third the symbol
rate of the channel.* The channel capacity of such a channel is
only .635 bit per symbol, so the efficiency is about

$$\frac{R}{C} = \frac{.333}{.635} = .525$$

which is more than half.

The next section will show examples of analog modulation tech-
niques for improving the transmission efficiency of channels, but
none of them has an efficiency approaching this when the signal-
to-noise ratio is low. When a transmission channel is strained to
its utmost, when power is at a premium, when noise and interference override other considerations, a digital transmission system is capable of squeezing more out of a channel than we are
now able to do with analog means. An exception arises when we
can use the human brain as a decoder, as in telephone transmission
and television reception, where a human receptor can get reliable
communication out of a noisy channel. But even so, we appear to
be approaching the point where speech can be reduced to digits in
a form removing much of its redundancy and sent over a channel
of capacity so small that a conventionally modulated signal could
not be transmitted.

* K. E. Perry and J. M. Wozencraft, "SECO: A Self-Regulating Error Correcting Coder-Decoder," *International Symposium on Information Theory*,
Brussels, Belgium, September 3–7, 1962.

3.3   *Channel Capacity of Some Representative Channels*

Let us now compute the channel capacity of some typical transmission channels. First, what is the channel capacity of a 100-word-per-minute teletype (TTY) channel? This channel can transmit 600 letter or space characters per minute, or 10 characters per second. We saw before that the maximum information associated with 1 such character is 4.76 bits, so that the capacity of this channel is 47.6 bits per second — say 50 bits per second.

What is the channel capacity of an audio circuit for the transmission of speech? Being rather liberal, let us say that the signal-to-noise ratio P/N is 36 decibels, and that the bandwidth W is 4500 cycles per second. Such a channel is better than a telephone channel, and comparable to an AM broadcast radio channel. Working out the formula, we find that the channel capacity is 48,000 bits per second — let us say 50,000 bits per second.

What is the channel capacity of a channel used to transmit a video signal? Again being rather liberal, let us say that the signal-to-noise ratio P/N is 30 decibels, and that the bandwidth W is 5,000,000 cycles per second. Application of the formula in this case yields a channel capacity of 50,000,000 bits per second.

Thus, a voice circuit has about 1000 times the channel capacity of a teletypewriter channel, and a video circuit has about 1000 times the channel capacity of a voice circuit.

But is it possible to send the output of 1000 voice circuits through a single video channel, or to send the output of 1000 teletypewriter circuits through one voice channel? Not necessarily. As a matter of fact, many channels designed for video transmission will transmit very nearly 1000 voice circuits, but no one has ever squeezed 1000 teletypewriter channels into one voice channel of the kind just described and we do not expect that anyone ever will accomplish this feat. We are usually satisfied to get 16 teletype channels into such a voice circuit, but sometimes use more elaborate equipment to get 48 circuits. By the use of extremely elaborate terminal equipment, we appear to be able to get 100 or even 200 teletype channels into such a voice circuit.

There are three reasons for this limitation. First, an actual voice transmission channel usually is not an ideal channel in the sense we have described it: uniform, invariant with time, with no perturbation other than random noise. Most radio and telephone voice channels have distortion and nonrandom noise, such as interference and cross talk, but of a nature which does not interfere with human voice communication. These perturbations may disturb other kinds of signals, and hence effectively reduce the channel capacity. Second, when we deal with discrete signals, we normally have a very small signaling alphabet, and at the same time demand low error rates. For example, if we send in the form of pulses through an apparatus that detects the pulses one at a time, so that $v = 1$, about 5 pulses are required for each character; and if we require a character error rate of less than 10^{-4}, then the error rate for an individual pulse must be $P(e) \leq 2 \times 10^{-5}$. Solving the above equation of the previous section for R/C gives $R/C \sim .03$; that is, the number of teletype channels which could be multiplexed through one voice channel is about $.03 \times 1000 = 30$. This value compares reasonably well with the observed value of 16, especially when we consider that the voice circuit for which the teletype multiplexer must be designed is usually a marginally satisfactory circuit having lower signal-to-noise ratio and smaller bandwidth than the audio circuit described above. This consideration does not prevail in converting from television to voice and back, for the human listener does not decode the speech one bit at a time. He rather listens for whole phonemes, syllables, words, and even sentences before committing himself finally to a decision about what he has just heard.

Third, there is some loss, nevertheless, when a large channel is subdivided, just as wood is wasted when a tree is sawed into planks. However, in a system (such as the Bell System L-3 cable carrier transmission system) which is designed to carry voice or television signals, the trade-off is at the rate of 600 to 800 voice channels per television channel, and most of the remaining discrepancy is accounted for by "guard bands," empty bands of frequency inserted between adjacent channels to make channel separation easier at the terminals.

Let us recapitulate briefly. We have defined quantity of information, and the rate at which information is generated by a discrete source. We have computed the information generated by certain kinds of sources. We have defined the channel capacity of a discrete channel. We have defined the channel capacity of a band-limited channel with Gaussian white noise, and used the definition to compute the channel capacity of certain kinds of channels. We have stated in loose form a theorem about encoding, to the effect that any channel can transmit the information from a source which generates information at a rate less than the channel capacity of the channel.

Exercise

The Information Capacity of a Human Being

What is the capacity of a human being as a channel for information? A precise answer to this problem depends on a more detailed formulation of the problem, but even in such general terms quantitative limits can be set.

At the upper end, consider reading. A person can read several hundred words per minute of ordinary English text. (Although speed-readers can read several thousand words per minute, it seems they accomplish this by skipping.) Let us estimate a maximum of 500 words per minute without skipping. At 5 letters per word, 1 bit per letter, this corresponds to 42 bits per second. Carefully controlled psychological experiments give about the same result.

At the other extreme, consider the feats of Masters who are experts in simultaneous blindfold chess play. Such a player is able to keep track of approximately 40 games simultaneously, and can play them out in about 6 hours. Assuming 40 (double) moves per game, we discover that the Master learns one move every 14 seconds, well enough to carry on sophisticated strategy, and with a low enough cumulative error rate so that in most exhibitions the Master never becomes "confused."

But what is the bit content of a chess move? In most cases, the individual player's response, which is one-half move, probably contains more than 1 bit: He frequently has the choice of half a dozen good moves, rarely fewer than 2. For the bit content to be as low as $\frac{1}{2}$ bit, there must be one response whose probability is greater than 0.9 (see Figure 1.7). An analyst would probably call such a response "forced," and such situations do occur from time to time. For the bit content to exceed 4, the player must have available more than 16 equally probable moves or the equivalent. This is also rare. The range $\frac{1}{2}$ to 4 bits seems to cover most situations.

A further check is possible. A well-known collection of chess openings* contains 1215 different chess openings, exclusive of footnotes and annotations. A spot check of 10 master games† played in the year in which the collection of openings was published (necessary because published analyses of openings and openings in master tournaments are mutually influencing) shows that the median master game follows the published openings for $3\frac{1}{2}$ moves. This suggests that $3\frac{1}{2}$ moves hold about as many bits as a choice among 1215 openings, giving a figure of about 3 bits per move, or 1.5 bits per half-move. This is consistent with the above estimate. We can guess that the bit content increases as the game proceeds from the opening to the middle game, then decreases in the end game. (However, estimating the length of a chess game at 40 moves automatically eliminates most end games, which are likely to take place in moves 40 to 70 or so.)

If we take a figure of 3 bits per move, the Master at simultaneous blindfold chess is taking in .2 bit per second, and making full use of it.

Thus, we have the following rough estimates. A human being can absorb .2 bit per second for a period of many hours, keep track of it all, and make purposeful use of it. He can process with his eyes and mind about 40 bits per second, pay-

* Griffith and White, revised by Reuben Fine, *Modern Chess Openings*, sixth edition, David McKay, Philadelphia, 1939.

† Games 63–72 of *Keres' Best Games of Chess, 1931–40*, Fred Reinfeld, editor, David McKay, Philadelphia, 1942.

ing at least some attention to all of it and making some use
of it.

3.4 Comparison of Various Practical Communication Channels

Let us now go back to the formula expressing the channel
capacity of a band-limited noisy channel, and do some manipula-
tion with it.* For example, how much energy must be supplied
to transmit one bit of information:

Let

$$P = \text{signal spectral power density in watts per}$$
$$\text{cycle per second, or joules}$$
$$W = \text{signal bandwidth in cycles per second}$$

Observe that we are using not power in watts, but spectral power
density in watts per cycle per second. This is convenient because
in many practical cases we wish to consider the bandwidth W as
a parameter while keeping the spectral power densities fixed. With
this scheme of units

$$PW = \text{signal power in watts}$$

Since

$$C = \text{channel capacity in bits per second}$$

then

$$\frac{PW}{C} = \text{energy in joules per bit}$$

Using the formula above for channel capacity C, one finds

$$\frac{PW}{C} = N \frac{P/N}{\log (1 + P/N)}$$

where

$$N = \text{noise energy in watts per cycle per second}$$

In many practical situations, the noise energy per unit bandwidth

* The material in this section is borrowed largely from Reference 6 in the
Bibliography.

is physically traceable to thermal effects, and is related to temperature by the formula*

$$N = KT = 1.37 \times 10^{-23}\, T \text{ watt/cycle per second}$$

where K is Boltzmann's constant and T is the absolute temperature. This relation leads to the definition of an *effective temperature* or *noise temperature*

$$T_e = \frac{N}{K}$$

even when the actual noise N may not be of thermal origin.

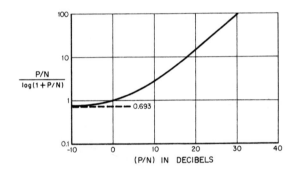

Figure 3.5   Normalized energy per bit required to signal over a noisy channel.

The number of joules required to transmit 1 bit is directly proportional to the noisiness or noise temperature of the channel, a relation which is quite understandable, and also to a certain function of the signal-to-noise ratio P/N. This function is plotted (Figure 3.5) as a function of the signal-to-noise ratio for easier analysis of its behavior. It is a steadily increasing function of P/N. Its minimum value is 0.693, which is approached when

---

* At very high frequencies quantum effects may make this model of noise inappropriate. See J. P. Gordon, "Quantum Effects in Communication Systems," *Proc. IRE, 50,* 1898–1908 (1962).

P/N is zero, that is, when the signal is very small compared to the noise. When the signal power density is as great as the noise power density, that is, when P/N equals 1, the value of this function has risen from 0.693 to unity. Beyond that point it rises very rapidly. For the signal-to-noise ratios that we like to think of in communications, 30 or 40 db, this function exceeds 100. The energy required to transmit 1 bit of information is 100 times greater when the signal-to-noise ratio is 30 decibels than when the signal-to-noise ratio is less than 0 decibels.

This observation is not new, but it still comes as a shock to a great many people. Many will insist that it is not in accordance with experience. Why do we persist in using communication systems which use so much more energy than necessary to transmit information?

There are three principal technical reasons why most communication systems do not approach this ideal.

First, the modulation system does not make efficient use of bandwidth in reducing power required.

Second, the signal in its original form does not make efficient use of the channel provided, that is, the signal characteristics and the channel characteristics are not well-matched.

Third, the information content of the signal is not commensurate with its characteristics. Most signals which it is desired to transmit contain a great deal of unnecessary detail, that is, they are greatly redundant. Redundancy may be useful, since it adds to the reliability, or accuracy of the message, but it is not usually present in a very efficient form.

All of these technical objections could be overcome or alleviated, at least in some degree, but the ultimate decision faced by the communications system engineer is based not on the desire to transmit a bit with the least possible amount of energy, but on the desire to satisfy a particular communication need at the minimum cost. In most communication systems designed in the past, the cost of power has not been one of the principal system costs. However, when power does become an important part of the cost of the communication system, the designers will be driven to systems which operate with broader bandwidth and lower signal-to-noise ratio, in order to make the best possible use of power.

In electronic systems involving the use of unattended equipment in satellites, power becomes an important factor because it must be generated by solar batteries or by some other relatively uneconomical means — uneconomical not only because of initial cost, but also because the power supply may take up a significant

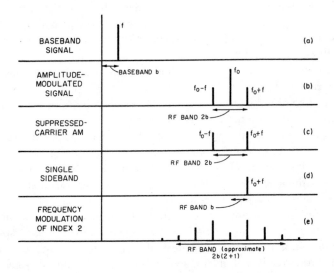

Figure 3.6   Spectrum of AM, suppressed-carrier, SSB, and FM waves when the baseband signal is a single cosinusoid.

part of the total available space and weight. In passive communication satellite experiments such as Project ECHO, power is once again one of the limiting factors in performance. There is good reason to believe, therefore, that designers of communication equipment for use in active and in passive satellite communication relay systems will try to exploit the advantages of broad bandwidth, low signal-to-noise-ratio communication in the future.

In sending signals by radio, we can use various systems of modulation. These require various bandwidths and powers, and have various advantages depending upon the signal characteristics and system requirements. Let us see how close they approach the ideal of using only $0.693N$ joule to send a bit.

We will consider first three comparatively well-known modulation schemes: single sideband modulation (SSB), frequency modulation (FM), and frequency modulation with feedback (FMFB).

In single sideband modulation (SSB), a constant radio frequency is added to all frequencies in the baseband (voice, TV, or other) signal. For example, a baseband signal $\alpha \cos 2\pi ft$ might be represented as a modulation wave $\alpha \cos 2\pi(f_0 + f)t$, where f_0 is the carrier frequency. Figure 3.6a and d illustrates the spectra of such signals. The rf bandwidth required is the same as the baseband bandwidth b. The signal-to-noise ratio in the recovered baseband signal is the same as the rf signal-to-noise ratio (assuming that no noise is added in amplification). That is,

$$\frac{S}{N} = \frac{P}{N}$$

where

S = baseband signal spectrum power density in watts per cycle per second (joules)

and P and N are defined as before. Thus

$$C = W \log\left(1 + \frac{S}{N}\right)$$

$$= W \log\left(1 + \frac{P}{N}\right)$$

and

$$\frac{PW}{C} = N\frac{P/N}{\log(1 + P/N)}$$

$$= (0.693N)\left[1.44\frac{P/N}{\log(1 + P/N)}\right]$$

The system is less efficient than the ideal by a factor

$$1.44\frac{P/N}{\log(1 + P/N)}$$

For output signal-to-noise ratios required for good quality speech or television, this factor makes the system several hundred times less efficient than the ideal. The main advantage of SSB is its economy of bandwidth.

In amplitude modulation (AM), the baseband signal $\alpha \cos 2\pi ft$ is represented by the modulated signal $(1 + \alpha \cos 2\pi ft)(\cos 2\pi f_0 t)$. By trigonometric identities this signal can be shown to be equal to

$$(\alpha/2) \cos 2\pi (f_0 - f)t + \cos 2\pi f_0 t + (\alpha/2) \cos 2\pi (f_0 + f)t$$

The AM spectrum is illustrated in Figure 3.6b. The constant carrier term $\cos 2\pi f_0 t$ can be removed by filtering to get a suppressed carrier AM signal, whose spectrum is illustrated in Figure 3.6c.

In AM, an rf band twice as big as the base bandwidth is required, because two sidebands are transmitted. At full modulation, AM requires three times as much power, and with ordinary signal statistics, many times as much power, as SSB. However, when the carrier is suppressed, the system has the same power requirement as SSB, but still requires twice the bandwidth. The chief advantage of AM over SSB is the circuit simplicity.

In frequency modulation, the baseband signal $\cos 2\pi ft$ is represented by the modulated signal

$$\cos (2\pi f_0 t + M \cos 2\pi ft)$$

This cannot be expressed as a finite number of cosinusoids. However, it can be expressed as

$$\sum_{n=-\infty}^{\infty} J_n(M) \cos [2\pi (f_0 + nf)t]$$

where $J_n(M)$ is the Bessel function of order n and argument M. This is illustrated in Figure 3.6e for $M = 2$. Now it is a mathematically valid and practically justifiable observation that when $|n| > M + 1$, $J_n(M)$ is very small, and we can ignore those components. This results in a practical estimate of rf bandwidth.

$$B = 2(M + 1)b$$

Another way of justifying this heuristically is to say that the instantaneous carrier frequency varies from $f_0 - Mf$ to $f_0 + Mf$

and carries with it a local sideband pattern of width $2b$, just as an AM signal does. The estimate is rough, but is amply justified by its practical usefulness and validity,

$$B = 2(\Delta f + b) = 2(M + 1)b$$

If (P/N) is the rf carrier-to-noise power ratio, the baseband signal-to-noise ratio (S/N) is

$$\frac{S}{N} = 3\left(\frac{P}{N}\right) M^2(M + 1)$$

This formula looks abstruse, and is somewhat difficult to derive, but it is really quite plausible, as can be seen from the following argument. Suppose we imagine a system in which the total transmitted power (carrier power) is fixed, but the modulation index M is variable. The output of the detector is a measure of the frequency deviation of the carrier, and its amplitude is therefore proportional to M. The signal power S therefore varies as M^2:

$$S \propto M^2$$

On the other hand, the spectral power density P of the transmitted signal is related to the carrier power P_c by

$$P = \frac{P_c}{B} = \frac{P_c}{2(M + 1)b} \propto \frac{1}{M + 1}$$

Hence

$$\frac{S}{P} \propto M^2(M + 1)$$

or

$$\frac{S}{N} \propto \frac{P}{N} M^2(M + 1)$$

There only remains the evaluation of the constant of proportionality. A more detailed analysis shows that the correct value is 3. The analysis is complicated by the fact that the demodulated noise spectrum density of an FM channel is not uniform, but is proportional to demodulated frequency.

For an FM detector system to work, it is necessary that the carrier amplitude be large in comparison with the noise amplitude.

It is not hard to see why: The discriminator must be able to follow unambiguously the coherent pattern of peaks and dips in the sinusoidally oscillating signal. If the noise is too big, a loop of the sinusoid will be canceled out from time to time, or an extra peak or dip added. Under these conditions, the discriminator will make an erroneous identification of phase and will skip or add an apparent full cycle. Practically speaking, this hazard is reduced to negligible proportions only if the carrier-to-noise ratio is at least

$$\frac{P}{N} = 16, \text{ or } 12 \text{ db}$$

As the index M is increased, the required rf bandwidth is increased; hence, the total rf noise is increased, and the minimum permissible transmitted power is increased. On the other hand, increasing the deviation makes the baseband signal-to-noise ratio greater than the carrier-to-noise ratio.

The channel capacity at minimum power level is

$$C = b \log \left(1 + \frac{S}{N} \right)$$

$$= b \log \left[1 + 48M^2(1 + M) \right]$$

Hence, the energy per bit is

$$\frac{PB}{C} = (0.693N) \frac{46(1 + M)}{\log \left[1 + 48M^2 (1 + M) \right]}$$

The energy is greater than the ideal of $.693N$ by a factor

$$\frac{46(1 + M)}{\log \left[1 + 48M^2 (1 + M) \right]}$$

This factor has an optimum value of about 15, consistent with an index M of 2 and an output S/N of 600 or 27 db. Thus, ordinary FM is at best about 15 times less efficient in the use of power than the ideal. The efficiency of FM is relatively insensitive to variation of index M from 1 to 4. The corresponding range of signal-to-noise ratios is 20 to 35 db. This range is of considerable practical interest for voice and many other analog signals.

Figure 3.7 shows a block diagram of frequency modulation with feedback, also called the Chaffee system or FMFB.

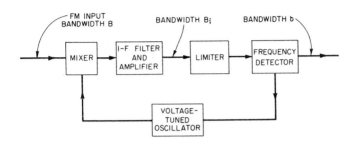

Figure 3.7   Frequency modulation with feedback (FMFB):
block diagram of a detector.

In an FMFB system, we use the output of the discriminator to cause a beating oscillator partially to track changes in carrier frequency. Of course, it cannot track perfectly, for in that case the output of the mixer would have constant frequency and there would be no signal for the discriminator to detect. However, if a frequency change δf at the detector causes a change $\mu \delta f$ in the voltage tuned oscillator, then the deviation M_i in the intermediate frequency amplifier is reduced to

$$M_i = \frac{M}{1 + \mu}$$

Here μ is completely analogous to the gain in the feedback loop of a linear amplifier, and the amount of feedback in decibels is

$$\text{feedback} = 20 \log_{10} \mu \text{ db}$$

Thus we can cut down the intermediate frequency bandwidth B_i to a value

$$B_i = 2\left(\frac{M}{1 + \mu} + 1\right) b$$

Inasmuch as the IF bandwidth is less than the total rf bandwidth,

the noise in the IF band is less than that in the rf band. We will
still need a 12-db carrier-to-noise ratio at the discriminator, but
the rf carrier-to-noise ratio can be less by the ratio of the IF
bandwidth to the rf bandwidth.

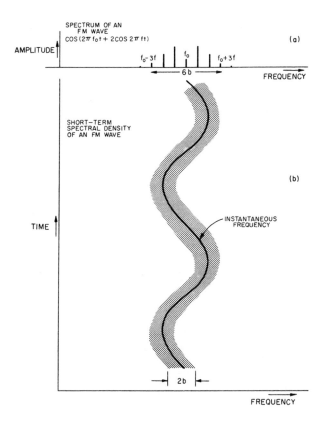

Figure 3.8 Spectrum and short-time spectral density of an FM wave.

Another way of expressing this idea is illustrated in Figure 3.8.
The spectrum of the FM wave, as described before, extends from
$f_0 - 3f$ to $f_0 + 3f$. This spectrum is illustrated in Figure 3.8a.

However, over a short period of time an investigation of spectral energy density will show the energy to be concentrated about the instantaneous frequency in a band of breadth about $2b$. This is depicted in Figure 3.8b. A filter of bandwidth $2b$ located at the right center frequency would pass almost all the signal energy. The effect of the feedback loop in the detector is to shift the effective center frequency of the IF filter almost in synchronism with the instantaneous frequency of the incoming carrier.

The minimum allowable signal-to-noise ratio now becomes

$$\frac{PB}{NB_i} = 16$$

An analysis like the one performed above leads to a required energy per bit of

$$\frac{PB}{C} = 0.693 \, \frac{46[M/(1 + \mu) + 1]}{\log \{1 + 48M^2[1 + M/(1 + \mu)]\}}$$

This energy is greater than the ideal by a factor

$$\frac{46[M/(1 + \mu) + 1]}{\log \{1 + 48M^2[1 + M/(1 + \mu)]\}}$$

This expression is only approximate, because when M is very large, the minimum allowable discriminator signal-to-noise ratio is greater than 12 decibels. When this is accounted for, this factor is found to go asymptotically to a theoretical value of 2 as M is increased. Experimentally, it appears that one can achieve a value of about 3, that is, that one can operate with only three times the minimum theoretical power requirement given by information theory.

That is, it is possible to receive information with a receiver power of:

$$P = 3(0.693)CN$$

$$= 3(0.695)CKT_e \text{ watts}$$

where T_e is the effective noise temperature, and K is Boltzmann's constant.

Phase lock reception is similar to the foregoing system except that the local oscillator is in effect made to track the received signal in phase.

Some pulse transmission systems, such as pulse position modulation, appear to be capable of as great a power efficiency as FMFB. Whether or not they are competitive will depend upon equipment economy and, in some cases, upon the kind of information that is to be transmitted.

It should be noted that the channel capacities attributed to various modulation systems above are not binary digit signaling rates. We have accepted at face value the value which the channel capacity formula gives for the demodulated baseband channel, and compared that with the rf power. This comparison is still fair, however, if we are dealing exclusively with analog channels.

4

Detection as a Communication Process

4.1 Representation of Band-Limited Functions
on an Orthogonal Basis

Detection of a signal such as a radar echo in a background of noise may be treated as a communication process also. Suppose, for example, a situation exists where a signal $s(t)$ may or may not be present in a background of noise $n(t)$. Let us suppose for illustration that the noise is Gaussian with a uniform power density spectrum N up to a maximum frequency W, that the signal falls in the same frequency range, and that our observation is limited to the period of time $0 \leq t \leq T$, which is supposed to include all of the nonzero part of the signal $s(t)$.

Using the sampling theorem as before, we can represent the signal by a point in $2WT$-dimensional space. It is convenient to make a slight scale change and represent a function $f(t)$ by*

$$f(t) = \sum_{k=1}^{2TW} f_k \phi_k(t)$$

where

$$\phi_k(t) = \sqrt{2W} \, \frac{\sin 2\pi W(t - k/2W)}{2\pi W(t - k/2W)}$$

$$f_k = \frac{1}{\sqrt{2W}} \, f\!\left(\frac{k}{2W}\right)$$

Figures 4.1 and 4.2 show graphically how a function $f(t)$ is built up of such elements ϕ. It is not hard to show that the set of func-

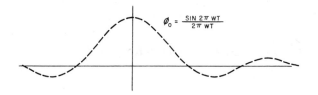

$$\phi_0 = \frac{\text{SIN } 2\pi \text{ WT}}{2\pi \text{ WT}}$$

Figure 4.1   A pulse for constructing band-limited functions from equally spaced samples.

tions $\phi_k(t)$ are orthogonal and normal, i.e., that

$$\int_{-\infty}^{\infty} \phi_k(t)\phi_l(t) \, dt = \begin{cases} 0 \text{ if } k \neq l \\ 1 \text{ if } k = l \end{cases}$$

Given two functions $f(t)$ and $g(t)$, we can define a scalar product

$$f(t) \cdot g(t) = \sum_{1}^{2TW} f_k g_k$$

From the foregoing integral relation it follows that

* Unless otherwise indicated all sums are over the range $(1,2TW)$ and all integrals over the range $(-\infty, \infty)$.

$$\int_{-\infty}^{\infty} f(t)g(t)\ dt = \int_{-\infty}^{\infty} \sum f_k\phi_k(t) \sum g_l\phi_l(t)\ dt = \sum_1^{2TW} f_k g_k$$

which provides an alternative formula for the scalar product. Following this notation we let

$$s(t) = \sum s_k\phi_k,\ n(t) = \sum n_k\phi_k$$

We may call the total signal energy S, and we see that, in suitable units,

$$\int s^2(t)\ dt = S = \sum s_k^2$$

The total noise energy is the product of noise spectral density bandwidth, and time.

$$NWT = \int n^2(t)\ dt = \sum n_k^2$$

The expected value of n_k^2 for any k is therefore $N/2$. To avoid a sticky problem, we can assume the noise sample amplitudes n_k

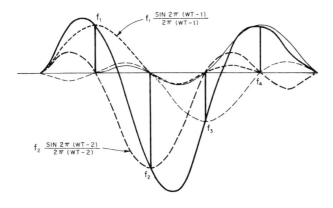

Figure 4.2   A band-limited function synthesized from samples, using the pulse of Figure 4.1.

have expected value zero and variance $N/2$ and that they are independent and normally distributed. (See the next exercise.)

This is a satisfactory definition of white Gaussian noise of power density spectrum N and bandwidth W.

Exercise

A Note on Probability Distribution

In dealing with collections of numbers having properties randomness, such as observations of electrical noise, it is convenient to introduce certain concepts from statistical analysis. In particular, let us assume we have a collection of numbers x_1, x_2, x_2, ..., x_N, and define the following:

$$m = \text{the mean} = \frac{1}{N} \sum_{j=1}^{N} x_j$$

$$s^2 = \text{the variance} = \frac{1}{N} \sum_{j=1}^{N} s_j^2 - m^2$$

The mean is what we call in plain language the average. The variance is more esoteric: The square root of the variance, s, is called the standard deviation, and is a measure of the extent to which the numbers x_j scatter from the mean value m.

Under many circumstances the set of N numbers is taken from a much larger or infinite set, called the population. This set of N numbers is then called a sample. The population mean μ and population variance σ^2 are defined just as the sample mean m and variance s^2. If necessary, limiting operations are used. If the number of elements N in the sample is large, we are often justified in treating the sample mean m and variance s^2 as about equal to the population mean μ and variance σ^2.

If each element x_m of the population is the sum of a large number of statistically independent numbers, then (with certain technical restrictions) the distribution of values of the elements x_m will approach a particular distribution, called the Gaussian or normal distribution, characterized thus: In any random sample of N elements, the number of elements having a value between x_0 and $x_0 + \Delta x$ is approximately

$$NP\left(\frac{x_0 - \mu}{\sigma}\right)\frac{\Delta x}{\sigma}$$

where $P(u)$ is the normal probability distribution function

$$P(u) = \frac{1}{\sqrt{2\pi}}\,e^{-\mu^2/2}$$

The normal probability distribution has been extensively studied, and is a satisfactory model for a wide variety of statistical phenomena. Sums and differences of normally distributed independent numbers are also normally distributed. For example, we can take sums of the elements x_n M at a time, thus

$$y_0 = \sum_1^M x_n, \; y_1 = \sum_{M+1}^{2M} x_n, \; y_k = \sum_{kM+1}^{(k+1)M} x_n$$

Then the population of all possible values of y_k has a mean $M\mu$ and a variance $M\sigma^2$. This and other properties of normal distributions will be referred to often in the next sections, and are described and proved in texts on probability.

4.2 Signal-to-Noise Ratio Required for Reliable Detection

Now let us consider the detection problem where the noise field $n(t)$ is present, and the signal $s(t)$ may or may not be present. We observe a received signal $f(t)$ where

$$f(t) = s(t) + n(t) = \sum(s_k + n_k)\phi_k \text{ when the signal is present}$$
$$= n(t) \qquad\qquad = \sum n_k\phi_k \qquad \text{when the signal is absent}$$

Figure 4.3a and b illustrates a pair of such waveforms. When no signal is present, the expected value of each coordinate f_k is zero, and its variance is $N/2$. When the signal is present, the expected value of f_k is s_k, and the variance is still $N/2$.

Now we introduce the geometrical concept of rotation of coordinates. The probability distribution of our observations is spherically symmetrical with respect to their centers, and hence retains the same form with a rotation of axes, that is, the proba-

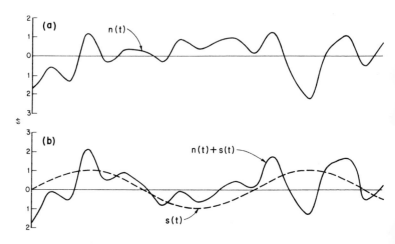

Figure 4.3   Noise $n(t)$ with and without a low-level signal $s(t)$.

bility distribution of the new coordinate will still be normal with variance $N/2$ regardless of the new directions of the axes.

For skeptics, we shall illustrate these concepts for the simplest nontrivial case, two dimensions. Suppose x and y are given, statistically independent, with normal distribution about 0 with variance $N/2$. Rotate the coordinate axes by an angle θ. Then

$$u = x \cos \theta + y \sin \theta$$

$$v = -x \sin \theta + y \cos \theta$$

Let us look now at the mean* and variance of u:

$$\bar{u} = \overline{x \cos \theta + y \sin \theta} = \bar{x} \cos \theta + \bar{y} \sin \theta = 0$$

$$\overline{u^2} = \overline{(x \cos \theta + y \sin \theta)^2} = \overline{x^2 \cos^2 \theta + 2xy \sin \theta \cos \theta + y^2 \sin^2 \theta}$$

$$= \left(\frac{N}{2}\right) \cos^2 \theta + \left(\frac{N}{2}\right) \sin^2 \theta + \overline{xy} \cdot 2 \sin \theta \cos \theta$$

* A horizontal bar over an expression signifies an average taken over a suitable range, usually an average over the statistical ensemble or a time average. Under a wide range of circumstances of interest (those satisfying *ergodic* conditions), the ensemble average and the time average are equal.

Note that the assumption that x and y are independent means simply that $\overline{xy} = \bar{x}\,\bar{y}$, which implies $\overline{xy} = 0$. Hence

$$\overline{u^2} = \frac{N}{2}$$

$$s^2 = \overline{u^2} - \bar{u}^2 = \frac{N}{2}$$

Similarly, the variance of v is $N/2$. Finally, u and v are statistically independent, for

$$\overline{uv} = \overline{(x \cos\theta + y \sin\theta)(-x \sin\theta + y \cos\theta)}$$

$$= \overline{(-x^2 + y^2)} \sin\theta \cos\theta = 0$$

Return now to the received signal $f(t)$, and let us choose a new set of coordinates so that one of the axes is parallel to $s(t)$. Let the basis for the new coordinate system be ψ_k, $k = 1, \cdots, 2TW$, and let the coordinates on the new basis be distinguished with primes ($'$). The representation of $s(t)$ in the new coordinate system will consist of one term

$$s(t) = \sqrt{S}\,\psi_1$$

so that obviously

$$\psi_1 = \frac{1}{\sqrt{S}}\, s(t)$$

The noise is represented by

$$n(t) = \sum_{x=1}^{2WT} n_k{'}\,\psi_k$$

Our problem is now that of distinguishing between

$$f(t) = s(t) + n(t) = (\sqrt{S} + n_1{'})\psi_1 + \sum_{2}^{2TW} n_k{'}\,\psi_k, \text{ signal present}$$

$$= n(t) = n_1{'}\,\psi_1 + \sum_{2}^{2TW} n_k{'}\,\psi_k, \text{ signal absent}$$

Obviously, there is no point in examining any term but the first. We can isolate the coefficient of the first function, ψ_1, by using scalar products.

$$f_1 = f(t) \cdot \psi_1(t) = \int_{-\infty}^{\infty} f(t)\psi_1(t) \, dt = \frac{1}{\sqrt{S}} \int_{-\infty}^{\infty} f(t)s(t) \, dt$$

and test the hypothesis

$$f_1 = \sqrt{S} + n_1{}', \text{ signal present}$$

against

$$f_1 = n_1{}', \text{ signal absent}$$

We know that $n_1{}'$ is normally distributed about zero with variance $N/2$ just like any among the original components n_k, for we assumed a pure rotation of the coordinate system (even though we never explicitly found the new coordinate system). The two distributions are illustrated in Figure 4.4. The problem is reduced

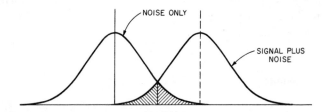

Figure 4.4   Probability distribution of output of a coherent detector whose input consists of waveforms like those in Figure 4.3.

to that of identifying the quantity $\sqrt{S}$ when perturbed by a noise with variance $N/2$. The ratio of the signal to the standard deviation of the noise is

$$d = \frac{\sqrt{S}}{\sqrt{N/2}} = \sqrt{\frac{2S}{N}}$$

For reliable detection d must be somewhat greater than unity. If the probability that $s(t)$ will be present is about 50 per cent,

TABLE 4.1

Probability of False Alarm Error and of Miss Error as a Function of Threshold
Level and Signal-to-Noise Ratio

$d = \sqrt{2S/N}$	Threshold					
	$\frac{1}{2}\sqrt{S}$		$\sqrt{S} - \sqrt{N/2}$		$\sqrt{S} - 2\sqrt{N/2}$	
	FA	Miss	FA	Miss	FA	Miss
4	2.3×10^{-2}	2.3×10^{-2}	1.4×10^{-3}	1.6×10^{-1}	2.3×10^{-2}	2.3×10^{-2}
5	6.2×10^{-3}	6.2×10^{-3}	3.2×10^{-5}	1.6×10^{-1}	1.4×10^{-3}	2.3×10^{-2}
6	1.4×10^{-3}	1.4×10^{-3}	2.9×10^{-7}	1.6×10^{-1}	3.2×10^{-5}	2.3×10^{-2}
7	2.3×10^{-4}	2.3×10^{-4}	2.0×10^{-9}	1.6×10^{-1}	2.9×10^{-7}	2.3×10^{-2}
8	3.2×10^{-5}	3.2×10^{-5}	2.6×10^{-12}	1.6×10^{-1}	2.0×10^{-9}	2.3×10^{-2}

and the penalty for missing it when it is present (which we call
miss) is the same as the penalty for detecting it when it is not
present (which we call false alarm or FA), then we would probably put the threshold of detection near $\frac{1}{2}\sqrt{S}$. This makes the
error probability the same for the two circumstances. They are
shown in the first two columns of Table 4.1. In a true search
situation, we are searching for a "needle in a haystack," and the
signal is expected to be absent nearly always. Cutting down the
false alarm rate becomes an operational problem, and it is advan-
tageous to raise the threshold. The table shows two examples.

In any case, a value of d of about 8 is needed, and we can say
roughly

$$\sqrt{\frac{2S}{N}} \sim 8$$

$$\frac{2S}{N} \sim 64$$

$$\frac{S}{N} \sim 32$$

$$S \sim 32N$$

Let us compare that practical signal-to-noise ratio with the ideal case. Suppose we are concerned with a detection scheme in which there are 1,000,000 cells to look in. If we look and find something, then we have potentially distinguished among about 10^6 possibilities, and receive potentially about 20 bits. We shall, therefore, expect to need

$$S = 20 \times 0.693N = 13.9N$$

in signal energy.

However, there is error rate to consider. In a detection process, a rather liberal error rate is allowable, say $P(e) \sim .01$. Referring to the previously quoted formula

$$P(e) \sim 2^{-\nu \alpha C/R}$$

we recall that 2^ν is the number of binary digits constituting a message; by analogy, $\nu = 20$. Solving for R/C, one finds

$$\frac{R}{C} \sim 0.41$$

Hence, the amount of energy required in the signal to achieve an error rate of 0.01 is really

$$S = 20 \times \frac{0.693N}{0.41} = 33N$$

This agrees very well with the value $32N$ derived above. The agreement is not fortuitous: This case fits the hypothesis of Fano's model quite precisely.

Notice that an error probability of 0.01 still requires a low false alarm rate: for the probability of a single false detection to be .01 in 10^6 cells, the probability of a false alarm in each cell must be less than 10^{-8}.

We see, therefore, that coherent detection, where viewed as a communication process, achieves about as much as one could expect. We need not look for new principles which will enable us to detect signals having less energy, but can devote ourselves to applying the conceptions of coherent detection and to engineering improvements to make the performance of such detectors live up to their design conception.

We can, of course, deliberately use a scheme like the one described earlier as a communication scheme. In such a case, it is usually impractical to search for one among a large number of signals. Costas* has described a system in which one of two signals, $+s(t)$ or $-s(t)$, is sent. Each one is "noiselike" in the sense of having no systematic pattern like a modulated carrier. The probability of error is

$$P(e) = \frac{2^{-C/R}}{2\sqrt{\pi(\log 2)\,C/R}}$$

when the signal-to-noise ratio is low. For $P(e) = 10^{-6}$, $C/R \simeq 16$. This code is an instance of orthogonal codes modified for symmetry about the origin, mentioned in a previous chapter, and the estimates of error probability agree.

4.3   Alerted and Unalerted Detection

It was casually implied above that a false alarm rate of 10^{-8} or so is desirable for unalerted detection in a search problem. This seems like an extraordinarily low rate of false alarms. Why is such a low rate desirable? The answer lies in the implicit difference between *search* and *demodulation:* the same mathematical description fits both, yet we sense that they differ.

The difference between search and demodulation is in the probability distribution of expected results. In a demodulation problem, we anticipate that the probability is distributed more or less uniformly among the two or more distinguishable outcomes. In a search problem, it is anticipated that one outcome, "nothing," has probability nearly unity, and that the probabilities of other possible outcomes are nearly infinitesimal.

Let us take an idealized example: Imagine a search radar, seeking aircraft. Suppose it has a range of 100 miles, a pulse bandwidth of 10 megacycles per second, an angular resolution of $\frac{1}{2}$ degree, and scans a sector of 2000 square degrees once every 2 seconds.

* J. P. Costas, "Poisson, Shannon, and the Radio Amateur," *Proc. IRE*, 47, 2058–2068 (1959).

If full use is made of the 10 megacycles per second bandwidth with a coherent detector the output of the detector will have a duration of about 10^{-7} second, more or less, depending on the precise pulse spectrum. As far as the simple detector is concerned, two events more than 10^{-7} second apart must be counted as independent. The 100-mile beam takes over 10^{-3} second to return. Hence, there is an opportunity for 10^4 independent events in each beam. Furthermore, scanning 2000 square degrees with a resolution of $\frac{1}{2} \times \frac{1}{2}$ degree implies about 8000 more or less independent beams. Therefore, in each complete scan, the number of opportunities for independent events, which is the number of cells which must be searched, is 8000×10^4 — roughly 10^8. Now, the actual number of targets actually anticipated is probably not more than 10, or at most 100. Hence, the probability of seeing a target in any one of the search cells is less than .000001, and the probability of seeing nothing is greater than .999999. In fact, in ordinary operation, many hours of scanning are likely for a few minutes of detection, and the probability of seeing a target is more likely to be about 10^{-8} or 10^{-9}.

In order to decide where to set the threshold, it is necessary to acknowledge that a false alarm costs something. For the sake of argument, let us suppose that each false alarm requires some response, say the attention of an operator for a few seconds with some resulting action, at a cost which can be measured at 1 cent. Suppose the false alarm rate is 10^{-7}. Then, a false alarm will pop up about 10 times every 2 seconds, 150,000,000 times per year, at a cost of $1,500,000 per year for false alarms only. The price is exorbitant: The false alarm rate must be made lower.

The foregoing example is purely fictitious and does not correspond to any real radar or any real search problem. The figures are typical of any true search problem, and the result is always the same; if the false alarm costs anything at all, even 1 cent, the tolerable false alarm rate is infinitesimal. Fortunately, as we have seen, the false alarm rate in a background of Gaussian noise can be reduced from 10^{-3} to 10^{-12} by a 6-db increase in signal-to-noise ratio.

Once an initial detection has been made, then the situation is different, because the *a priori* probabilities of seeing something and seeing nothing are no longer so unequal. We fully expect to see something with relatively few observations, and the situation is more like demodulation again, with a higher allowable false alarm rate.

Suppose, for example, that one radar like the one above makes a detection, and another attempts to locate the same object. The second radar may expect to look, say, over a 10-mile range interval in a solid angle 2 degrees square. The number of independent looks is around 10^4. Furthermore, a substantial false alarm rate is tolerable for a short period. The over-all effect is an increase of 3 or 4 orders of magnitude in the tolerable false alarm rate. The effect of this is to allow a reduction of the detection threshold by 3 or 4 db.

In an extreme case, the problem may be to confirm the existence of a particular event in a single particular observation, and the alerted operator has essentially only one single independent observation. Here a false alarm rate of .01 may be quite acceptable. Under these circumstances, the threshold can be lowered 6 to 8 db. It is worth noting that the penalty for false alarm may seem to be less in alerted detection, for if the alarm is false, the whole burden of responsibility may be borne by the initial (unalerted) detector rather than by the subsequent alerted detector.

In summary, according to this particularly simple model, the detection threshold should be 3 to 8 db lower for alerted detection than for unalerted detection. The exact figure depends on the penalty for false alarm and the nature of the search situation.

Exercise

Where Is the Information Located?

When the *information generated by a source* was defined, some pages back, we had in mind a source which turned out a stream of symbols or waveforms of comparable significance and roughly equal probabilities, and, without making an issue of it, we assumed that "information" flowed out at a steady rate, so many bits per symbol. When we carry out a search, however, we no longer have the feeling that every observation is equally important. *A priori* we cannot, of course, distinguish one from another; but after the observation is made, we are likely to consider it unimportant if nothing was observed, but very important if something was detected. Is this reflected in the mathematical description of the information flow?

There is one straightforward way to identify information with a particular message. If a particular message m_i in the ensemble of messages has probability p_i, then define its information as

$$h_i = -\log p_i$$

Then the average information, weighted, of course, to allow for the respective probabilities of the various messages, is

$$\sum p_i h_i = \sum -p_i \log p_i = H$$

which is just the information rate of the source.

According to this definition, in a search where the probability of seeing nothing in a particular observation is .999 999, the information delivered when nothing is seen is

$$-\log_2 .999999 = .00000144 \text{ bit}$$

while the information delivered when something is observed is

$$-\log_2 .000001 = 19.9 \text{ bits}$$

This way of attributing information to particular messages is open to a number of objections. The whole concept of *information* is based on looking forward to a message as yet unknown, not backward upon a known message. After a message has occurred, its probability is unity and the probability of any other message occurring in its place is zero. Before the message has occurred, the most we can expect from it is that it may resolve the uncertainty about what message may come: This uncertainty exists before the message comes, and is not a consequence of the particular message. In conducting a search, we are uncertain before each observation whether there is or is not a target to be seen there. After the observation, we know. The *information* in the observation is a direct measure of the uncertainty, in a precise statistical sense, which is removed by making the observation. How can we decree *after* the observation that this was different in the one case from the other?

However, the value of an idea is judged by its usefulness, not by how well it fits into the logical framework of our previous knowledge. Relativity and quantum mechanics are important instances of useful theories which contradicted accepted ideas of their time.

The preceding formula for the information in a specific message has not, to the best of my knowledge, been usefully applied anywhere in communication science. However, something analogous has been identified in a recent study of musical meaning.* The author distinguishes two kinds of events, normal or ordinary events representing some standard or the application of some set of rules, and exceptional events, which deviate from the standard or break the rules. He puts forward (among others) the thesis that meaning in music is carried by the exceptional events, and that the normal events are significant only in that they provide the standard of comparison against which the others are judged to be exceptional. The analogy to our search situation is clear.

This thesis was put forward without any formulas and, I suspect, in ignorance of what is today called information theory. Professor Meyer might even find my formulation obscure. (I pray he would not find that I have misinterpreted his intention.) Nevertheless, it winds in and out through many chapters of his book and is put to good use in his search for objective signs of meaning in music and the relation this meaning has to emotion. As a result, I am a good deal less confident that it is absurd to divide the information in a source into little packages and associate each package with a particular message. Perhaps some imaginative philosopher may show us the way to do this without becoming enmeshed in a web of contradictions and inconsistencies.

*Leonard B. Meyer, *Emotion and Meaning in Music*, University of Chicago Press, Chicago, 1956.

5

Coherent and Incoherent Integration

5.1 *Some Common Detectors*

In a communication system, the alphabet of transmission signals will ordinarily be chosen so that one or another reasonably efficient demodulation process can be used. As we have seen, the efficiency of a detection system may be analyzed with the same mathematical tools. However, the designer of a detection system may not be able to control the signal or the environment enough to approach an optimum or efficient modulation scheme. An important example is that of a search process where the signal to be detected lasts a very long time, and where knowledge of its presence or absence is desired in a short time. This circumstance leads to the idea of detection in a fixed or limited time, or in the discrete case, of detection with a limited number of observations.

Heuristically, it is clear that increasing the observation time or the number of observations cannot decrease the certainty of detection, and should increase it. We are thus led to ask, how much is the detection process improved by increasing the observation time? We shall answer this question by suggesting a simple, plausible, and easily implemented criterion of effectiveness involving both observation time and signal-to-noise ratio, and show how increased observation time can be traded for decreased signal-to-noise ratio.

Suppose we have noise $n(t)$ of bandwidth W, with a flat spectrum and rms amplitude N. Suppose we have a signal of constant dc amplitude S. If the noise is present alone, the received waveform is

$$f(t) = n(t)$$

If the signal is present also, we have

$$f(t) = n(t) + S$$

An example of such signals is shown in Figure 5.1. In this example, $N = 1$, $S = 1$. We would like to examine the following common detection schemes

I. Correlation detector: $\int_0^T f(t) S\, dt$

II. Square-law detector: $\int_0^T f^2(t)\, dt$

III. Linear rectifier: $\int_0^T |f(t)|\, dt$

to find the relation among the signal-to-noise ratio S/N and the integration time T. When the idea of detection is not uppermost, the circuits that perform these functions are sometimes called demodulators instead of detectors.

First, use the sampling theorem to characterize $f(t)$ as a sequence

$$f_k = f(k/2W) \qquad k = 1, 2, \cdots, 2TW$$
$$n_k = n(k/2W)$$

Figure 5.1 shows how the samples are related to the continuous function $f(t)$. The various samples f_k are independent and have a Gaussian distribution with variance N^2 (to avoid another proof,

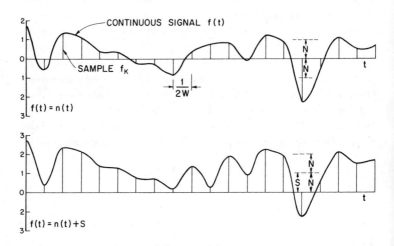

Figure 5.1   Random noise $n(t)$ with and without superimposed signal $s(t) = S$, showing samples.

we can *define* this as Gaussian white noise of bandwidth W). To a high degree of approximation, we can replace the integrals (with appropriate constant multiplying factors) by sums:

$$\text{I.} \quad S_I = \sum_1^{2TW} f_k \simeq \frac{2W}{S} \int_0^T [f(t)] S \, dt$$

$$\text{II.} \quad S_{II} = \sum_1^{2TW} f_k^2 \simeq 2W \int_0^T f^2(t) \, dt$$

$$\text{III.} \quad S_{III} = \sum_1^{2TW} |f_k| \simeq 2W \int_0^T |f(t)| \, dt$$

We shall devote the rest of the discussion to the sums S_I, S_{II}, and S_{III}, and try to see how they depend on the integration time and signal-to-noise ratio. The constant $2W$ or $2W/S$ is a scale factor and is not important for the present discussion.

5.2 Correlation Detector

Figure 5.2 shows the samples f_k, the squares of the samples $f_k{}^2$, and the absolute values of the samples $|f_k|$ for the noise, with and without signal, of Figure 5.1.

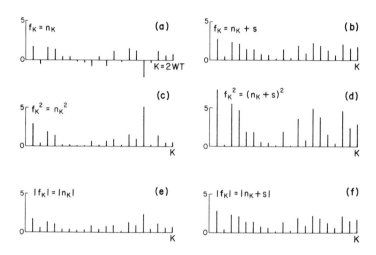

Figure 5.2 Samples, squares of samples, and absolute values of samples in the absence and in the presence of signals.

If we look at the signal $f(t)$ at any instant; that is, if we look at a single sample f_k, it has

$$\text{mean value } \mu_s = S, \text{ signal present}$$

$$\mu_0 = 0, \text{ signal absent}$$

$$\text{variance } \sigma_s{}^2 = N^2, \text{ signal present}$$

$$\sigma_0{}^2 = N^2, \text{ signal absent}$$

The two variances are the same, and we can ignore the distinction implied by the subscript. We can use $(\mu_s - \mu_0)/\sigma$ as a measure of effectiveness of a detection process. For a single sample of the

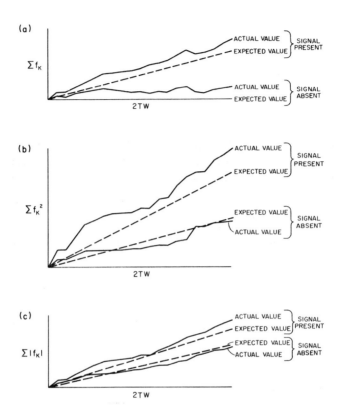

Figure 5.3 Σf_k, Σf_k^2, and $\Sigma |f_k|$ in the absence and in the presence of signals, compared with expected values.

signal, this is just the signal-to-noise ratio S/N. Figure 5.2a and b shows the samples f_k for the noise and for the signal plus noise shown in Figure 5.1. Figure 5.3 shows the sum

$$S_{\mathrm{I}} = \sum f_k = \sum (S + n_k)$$

as a function of $2TW$. The expected value of S_{I} is $\mu_s = 2TWS$ and its variance is

$$\sigma_s{}^2 = \left[\sum(S + n_k)\right]\left[\sum(S + n_j)\right] - (2TWS)^2$$
$$= \sum\sum(\overline{S^2} + \overline{Sn_j} + \overline{Sn_k} + \overline{n_k n_j}) - (2TWS)^2$$
$$= (2TW)^2 S^2 + 0 + 0 + \overline{\sum n_k{}^2} - (2TWS)^2$$
$$= \sum n_k{}^2$$
$$= 2TWN^2$$

Repeating the computation with $S = 0$, we find that the mean value and variance of $\sum n_k$ are $\mu_0 = 0$ and $\sigma_0 = 2TWN^2$.

Figure 5.4a and b illustrates the distribution of observations to be expected after integration over a time such that $2TW = 20$ and 100 respectively. The observations are distributed approximately in the well-known bell-shaped normal probability distribution. The center of the normal distribution curve is at the expected value μ, and the standard deviation is σ, the square root of the variance. In order to make an effective detector, it is necessary to set a threshold somehow so that an observation will nearly always fall on one side of the threshold when the signal is present, and nearly always fall on the other side of the threshold where the signal is absent. Inasmuch as the probability distributions overlap (the overlapping part is cross-hatched in the figure), there is no place to establish a threshold which will give error-free results. A reasonable and useful measure of the effectiveness is the ratio of the distance between the peaks, $\mu_s - \mu_0$, and the width of the peak, measured by σ. When only one sample is taken, we have seen that the ratio is S/N. When $2TW$ samples are integrated in a coherent detector, the measure of effectiveness is

$$\frac{\mu_s - \mu_0}{\sigma} = \frac{2TWS - 0}{\sqrt{2TWN^2}} = \sqrt{2TW}\,\frac{S}{N}$$

that is, the effect of integration over time T is equal to the effect of improving the S/N ratio by a factor $\sqrt{2TW}$.

5.3 *Square-Law Detector*

In a square-law detector, the sample is squared to get $f_k{}^2 = n_k{}^2$ or $(n_k + S)^2$ (Figure 5.2c and d). Let us examine the buildup of the sum,

$$S_{\text{II}} = \sum f_k{}^2 = \sum (S + n_k)^2$$
$$= \sum (S^2 + 2Sn_k + n_k{}^2), \text{ signal present}$$
$$\text{or } = \sum n_k{}^2, \text{ signal absent}$$

Its expected value is

$$2TWS^2 + 2TWN^2, \text{ signal present}$$

and

$$2TWN^2, \text{ signal absent}$$

Figure 5.3b shows the actual growth of $\sum f_k{}^2$ compared with the expected value, for both cases.

We could find the variance of S_{II} by brute force. However, it is easier to work indirectly, and to define a new population whose members are

$$z_k = S^2 + 2Sn_k + n_k{}^2$$

and find *sample mean* and *sample variance*, and work indirectly to the sums.

If we define

$$n_k = Nx_k$$

then x_k forms a normal population of variance unity, with a probability distribution

$$P(x) = \frac{1}{\sqrt{2\pi}} e^{-x^2/2} \, dx, \int_{-\infty}^{\infty} P(x) \, dx = 1$$

The mean value of $x_k{}^2$ is

$$\overline{x_k{}^2} = \int_{-\infty}^{\infty} x^2 P(x) \, dx = 1$$

The mean value of $x_k{}^4$ is

$$\overline{x_k{}^4} = \int_{-\infty}^{\infty} x^4 P(x) \, dx = 3$$

The mean values of x and x^3 are zero, because $P(x)$ is a symmetric (even) function. For n_k, the means are

$$\overline{n_k{}^2} = N^2$$

$$\overline{n_k{}^4} = 3N^4$$

Now for

$$S^2 + 2Sn_k + n_k{}^2$$

the mean value is

$$S^2 + \overline{2Sn_k} + \overline{n_k{}^2}$$

$$= S^2 + 0 + N^2$$

and the expected value of the sum is

$$\mu_s = \overline{\sum (s + n_k)^2} = 2TW(S^2 + N^2)$$

The variance of $(S + n_k)^2$ is

$$\overline{[(S + n_k)^2]^2} - \overline{(S + n_k)^2}{}^2$$

$$= \overline{S^4 + 4S^3n_k + 6S^2n_k{}^2 + 4Sn_k{}^3 + n_k{}^4} - (S^2 + N^2)^2$$

$$= S^4 + 0 + 6S^2N^2 + 0 + 3N^4 - S^4 - 2S^2N^2 - N^4$$

$$= 4S^2N^2 + 2N^4$$

Hence the variance of the sum is

$$\sigma_s{}^2 = 2TW(4S^2N^2 + 2N^4)$$

By repeating the computation with $S = 0$, we can find

$$\mu_0 = 2TWN^2$$

$$\sigma_0{}^2 = 2TWN^4$$

Figure 5.4c and d shows normal distribution curves with these means and variances for $2TW = 20$ and 100.

An aggravating factor here is that the variance is different when the signal is present than it is when the signal is absent. Let us agree that we are most interested in the case $S/N << 1$. Then

$$2TW(4S^2N^2 + 2N^4) \simeq 2TW \cdot 2N^4 = 4TWN^4$$

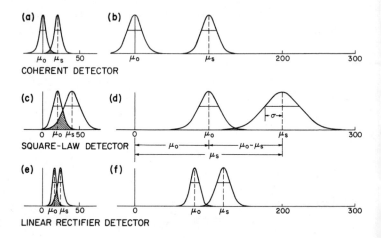

Figure 5.4   Distribution of observations for coherent, square-law, and
linear rectifier detection for two different integration times.
($2TW = 20$ for a, c, and e; $2TW = 100$ for b, d, and f.)

independent of whether the signal is present.

Using the same criterion as before, we measure the effectiveness
of the detector by

$$\frac{\mu_s - \mu_0}{\sigma} = \frac{2TW[(S^2 + N^2) - (N^2)]}{\sqrt{4TWN^4}} = \left(\frac{S}{N}\sqrt[4]{TW}\right)^2$$

that is, integrating a time T is equivalent to improving S/N by a
factor $\sqrt[4]{TW}$.

5.4   Linear Rectifier Detector

In a linear rectifier detector, the samples f_k are rectified to get
$|f_k| = |n_k|$ or $|n_k + S|$ (Figure 5.2c and f), and the detector output after integration is

$$S_{\text{III}} = \sum |f_k|$$

Once again we examine the individual terms of the sum, and ask, what are the mean and variance of $|f_k|$?

$$\overline{|f_k|} = \overline{|S + n_k|} = \overline{|S + Nx_k|}$$

$$= \frac{1}{\sqrt{2\pi}} \int_{-\infty}^{\infty} |S + Nx| e^{-x^2/2} dx$$

$$= \frac{1}{\sqrt{2\pi}} \int_{-\infty}^{x=S/N} - (S + Nx) e^{-x^2/2} dx$$

$$+ \frac{1}{\sqrt{2\pi}} \int_{-S/N}^{\infty} (S + Nx) e^{-x^2/2} dx$$

Here we can evaluate the integral approximately by a tedious but straightforward process, as follows:

Substitute

$$\int_{-\infty}^{0} + \int_{0}^{S/N} \text{ for } \int_{0}^{S/N} \text{ and analogously } \int_{S/N}^{0} + \int_{0}^{\infty} \text{ for } \int_{S/N}^{\infty}$$

Evaluate all integrals in $(0, \infty)$ and $(\infty, 0)$ exactly. Evaluate integrals in $(-S/N, 0)$ and $(0, S/N)$ by using the approximation

$$e^{-x^2/2} \simeq 1$$

The result is

$$\overline{|f_k|} \simeq \frac{2N}{\sqrt{2\pi}} \left(1 + \frac{S^2}{2N^2} \right), \quad \frac{S}{N} < 1$$

The expected value of the sum is

$$\mu_s = \overline{\sum |S + n_k|} \simeq \frac{2TW}{\sqrt{2\pi}} \left(2N + \frac{S^2}{N} \right)$$

when the signal is present, and

$$\mu_0 = \overline{\sum |n_k|} \simeq \frac{2TW}{\sqrt{2\pi}} 2N$$

when the signal is absent. The difference is

$$\mu_s - \mu_0 = \frac{2TW}{\sqrt{2\pi}} \cdot \frac{S^2}{N}$$

What about the variance? The mean square value is easy to evaluate; for the absolute value operation is trivial when the function is squared:

$$\overline{|S + n_k|^2} = \overline{(S + n_k)^2} = S^2 + N^2$$

One must be careful not to jump to conclusions, however. The mean value laboriously computed above must now be used.

$$\text{var}\,\{|S + n_k|^2\} = \overline{|S + n_k|^2} - [\overline{|S + n_k|}]^2$$

$$\simeq S^2 + N^2 - \frac{4N^2}{2\pi} - \frac{4S^2}{2\pi} - \frac{1}{2\pi}\frac{S^4}{N^2}$$

$$\sigma_s^2 \simeq 2TW \left[S^2 + N^2 - \frac{2N^2}{\pi} - \frac{2S^2}{\pi} - \frac{S^4}{2\pi N^2} \right]$$

If $S/N \ll 1$, this is approximately

$$\sigma_s^2 \simeq 2TWN^2 \left(1 - \frac{2}{\pi} \right)$$

Similarly

$$\sigma_0^2 \simeq 2TWN^2 \left(1 - \frac{2}{\pi} \right)$$

These probability distributions are plotted in Figure 5.4e and f for $2TW = 20$ and 100.

The measure of merit of the detector is

$$\frac{\mu_s - \mu_0}{\sigma} = \frac{2TWS \cdot (S/N)}{\sqrt{2\pi} \cdot \sqrt{2TW[1 - 2/\pi]} \cdot N}$$

$$= \left(\frac{S}{N} \sqrt[4]{\frac{TW}{\pi - 2}} \right)^2$$

that is, the effect of integration for a time T is equivalent to the effect of improving

$$\frac{S}{N} \text{ by a factor } \sqrt[4]{\frac{TW}{\pi - 2}}$$

Note that this is just a shade worse than $\sqrt{TW}$.
The ratio is $\sqrt[4]{1.00/1.1416}$ or approximately 0.1 decibel.

Exercise

Processing of Clipped Signals

Often it is inconvenient or expensive to process signals having a wide dynamic range, or it may be desirable to reduce the output of a process to a finite number of states for digital encoding. It is legitimate to ask what the penalty is.

The most extreme case possible is to reduce the output to two states. If the relation of input to output is as shown in Figure 5.5, this is called clipping.

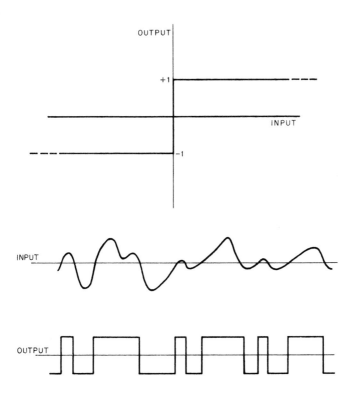

Figure 5.5   Relation of output to input in an ideal clipper.

Let us suppose we pass a wave $f(t)$ into the clipper, and suppose that $f(t)$ consists either of a noise $n(t)$, or of the same noise plus a known signal $s(t)$. Let us imagine, for instance, that $n(t)$ is a Gaussian, with uniform spectral density in the band of frequency $-W$ to W, and root-mean-square value N. Suppose that the value of $s(t)$ at a particular time t_0 is S. Let us look at the output of the clipper.

The distribution of

$$f(t_0) = S + n(t_0), \text{ signal present}$$

$$= n(t_0), \text{ signal absent}$$

is shown in Figure 5.6. The clipper output is $+1$ if $f(t_0) \geq 0$.

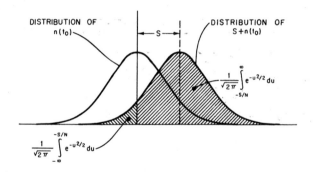

Figure 5.6   Distribution of $n(t_0)$ and $S + n(t_0)$.

When the signal is present, this happens when

$$S + n(t_0) \geq 0$$
$$n(t_0) \geq -S$$

That occurs with probability

$$P[n(t_0) \geq -S] = \frac{1}{\sqrt{2\pi N}} \int_{-S}^{\infty} e^{-u^2/2N^2} \, du$$

$$= \frac{1}{2} + \frac{1}{\sqrt{2\pi}} \int_{-S/N}^{0} e^{-u^2/2} \, du$$

For small values of S/N, we can expand $e^{-u^2/2}$ in power series and integrate to get

$$\frac{1}{\sqrt{2\pi}} \int_{-S/N}^{0} \left(1 - \frac{u^2}{2}\right) du = \frac{1}{\sqrt{2\pi}} \left[u - \frac{u^3}{6}\right]_{-S/N}^{0}$$

$$= \frac{1}{\sqrt{2\pi}} \left[\frac{S}{N} + \frac{1}{6}\left(\frac{S}{N}\right)^3\right]$$

$$P[f(t_0) \geq 0] = \frac{1}{2} + \frac{1}{\sqrt{2\pi}} \left[\frac{S}{N} + \frac{1}{6}\left(\frac{S}{N}\right)^3 + \cdots\right]$$

Similarly,

$$P[f(t_0) < 0] = \frac{1}{2} - \frac{1}{\sqrt{2\pi}} \left[\frac{S}{N} + \frac{1}{6}\left(\frac{S}{N}\right)^3 + \cdots\right]$$

If S_{out} is the output of the clipper, its expected value is

$$\mu_s = \overline{S_{\text{out}}} = 1 \cdot P[f(t_0) \geq 0] + (-1) \cdot P[f(t_0) < 0]$$

$$= \sqrt{\frac{2}{\pi}} \left[\frac{S}{N} + \frac{1}{3}\left(\frac{S}{N}\right)^3 + \cdots\right]$$

Noting that $S_{\text{out}}^2 = 1$ for any input, it is easy to find the variance

$$\sigma_s^2 = 1 - \frac{2}{\pi}\left(\frac{S}{N}\right)^2 + \cdots$$

When the signal is absent,

$$\mu_0 = 0$$

$$\sigma_0^2 = 1$$

When S/N is very small, we can ignore higher order terms and get

$$\frac{\mu_s - \mu_0}{\sigma} = \sqrt{\frac{2}{\pi}} \frac{S}{N}$$

This shows that the effective signal-to-noise ratio is reduced by $\sqrt{2/\pi}$, or about 1.9 decibels.

The loss is not entirely clearcut. We have lost 1.9 decibels according to a particular criterion, but at the clipper output we are no longer dealing with Gaussian noise of bandwidth W, nor is the noise even uncorrelated with the signal.

In fact, the clipping process makes the bandwidth of the clipper output greater than W, and over a period of time T we can integrate over more than $2TW$ samples to advantage. It has been shown that about 1.2 of the lost 1.9 decibels can be recovered if care is taken, and practical clipper detectors usually sample at time intervals of about $1/5W$ rather than $1/2W$.

5.5   *Comparison Among Detectors*

Table 5.1 summarizes the expected values and variances of the outputs of these three kinds of detectors. The effect of integration with a coherent detector over a time T is equivalent to an improvement in the input signal-to-noise ratio of a factor $\sqrt{2TW}$. This is sometimes stated as 3-decibel improvement per doubling of integration time. The effect of integration with an incoherent square-law or linear rectifier detector over a time T is equivalent (when the input S/N is low) to an improvement in the signal-to-noise ratio of $\sqrt[4]{TW}$ or $\sqrt[4]{TW/(\pi-2)}$ respectively. This is sometimes stated as 1.5-decibel improvement per doubling of integration time.

There is another respect in which the square-law and linear rectifier detectors are inferior to the coherent detector. The distributions in Figure 5.4 and in Table 5.1 show that the expected value of the output of a coherent detector depends on the signal only, and the variances on the noise only, whereas in square-law and linear rectifier detectors the expected values and variances depend jointly on signal and noise. Now to a first approximation, the best place to put the detection threshold depends on the expected value of the output, and not on the variance. This means that the threshold can be set in a coherent detector independent

TABLE 5.1

Expected Value and Variance of the Outputs of Several Types of Detectors

| | Noise Only | | Signal Plus Noise | |
	Expected Value	Variance	Expected Value	Variance
Coherent Detector	0	$2TWN^2$	$2TWS$	$2TWN^2$
Square-Law Detector	$2TWN^2$	$4TWN^4$	$2TW(S^2+N^2)$	$2TW(4S^2N^2+2N^4)$
Linear Rectifier Detector	$\dfrac{4TWN}{\sqrt{2\pi}}$	$2TWN^2\left(1-\dfrac{2}{\pi}\right)$	$\dfrac{2TW}{\sqrt{2\pi}}\left(2N+\dfrac{S^2}{N}\right)$	$2TW\left[(S^2+N^2)\left(1-\dfrac{2}{\pi}\right)-\dfrac{S^4}{2\pi N^2}\right]$

of the noise. This is not possible in linear or square-law detectors, for the output wanders back and forth as the noise level varies. Unless the noise is very uniform, as, for example, is thermal noise in a low-noise electronic amplifier, some extra provision must be made to compensate for secular variations in noise level.

These results were derived for a very particular signal waveform, a rectangular dc pulse. The conclusions are quite generally valid, however. The restriction to low input S/N is relatively unimportant in most practical cases, for the output signal-to-noise ratio improves monotonically with the input signal-to-noise ratio in all three of these detectors, and we can concentrate our attention on the "worst case," where the signal-to-noise ratio is as low as the system can stand.

What is the difference between coherent and incoherent detection? In the geometric language in which we represent each of a family of signals by a point in a space of $2WT$ dimensions, coherent detection makes use of the direction of the point relative to the coordinate axes as well as the distance, whereas incoherent detection uses the distance only.

Is there any detection which is "intermediate" between coherent and incoherent? Such systems have been described by

Jacobs* and others. In the system described by Jacobs, a band of the spectrum is divided into a number of discrete equal bands. The signal is made up of bursts of energy, not overlapping in time, and each is confined to one of the bands. Within each band, the energy is detected incoherently.

Let us examine why this is partly "coherent." Suppose the time duration of a burst is T, the total bandwidth is W, and the bandwidth of each of k bands is $W/k = B$. Let us imagine the signal represented not by its amplitude samples but by its frequency components.

$$f(t) = \sum_{n=1}^{TW} \left[a_n \cos\left(\frac{2\pi nt}{T}\right) + b_n \sin\left(\frac{2\pi nt}{T}\right) \right]$$

(For convenience, it is assumed that the signal lies in the band of frequency from 0 to W, but it could lie elsewhere with appropriate changes in representation.) The coefficients a_n and b_n are the coordinates, and the number of coordinates is $2TW$ (give or take a few, depending on whether we assume a dc term and whether TW is an integer or not).

Now let us look at a signal falling in a particular band, say

$$mB < f \leq (m+1)B$$

This is representable by

$$f(t) = \sum_{n=mBT+1}^{(m+1)BT} \left(a_n \cos\frac{2\pi nt}{T} + b_n \sin\frac{2\pi nt}{T} \right)$$

involving only $2BT$ terms. The receiver filters the incoming signal into a band $mB < f \leq (m+1)B$, and hence makes use of the fact that all components of $f(t)$ lie in a given subset of the possible directions. But after filtering, it uses an incoherent detector which makes no further use of the detailed relations among the components.

When the parameters are duly proportioned, this modulation

* I. Jacobs, "Optimum Integration Time for the Incoherent Detection of Noise-Like Communication Signals," presented at the 1962 Spring URSI Meeting, May 1; "The Asymptotic Behavior of Incoherent M-ary Communication Systems," *Proc. Inst. Elec. Electronics Engrs.*, 51, 250–251 (1963).

and detection scheme is reasonably efficient. In the band in which it falls, the transmitted signal should have a spectral power density about three times that of the noise for most efficient transmission. For most efficient performance, the number of bands, k, should be hundreds, and the information transmitted per burst is $\log_2 k$. The burst length is of the order of magnitude $20/B$, and the optimum is more or less dependent on the number of bands, k. The amount of power required per bit is about 60 $(0.693N)$ for $k = 2$ and falls to about 10 $(0.693N)$ for k of several hundreds. As the number of bands k approaches infinity, the amount of power required approaches the theoretical limit of $0.693N$. On this basis, it is competitive with AM, SSB, FM, and FM with feedback.

Why would such a modulation scheme be used? The detailed signal structure required for coherent detection is destroyed or degraded by such phenomena as Doppler shift, which obscures small frequency shifts, or multipath propagation, which destroys small time distinctions. With a signal in a band of total bandwidth kB and time duration $20/B$, we should require frequency discrimination approximating $B/20$ or time discrimination approximating $1/kB$ to make coherent detection possible, whereas this system operates with much coarser frequency bands of bandwidth B and much coarser time segments of length $20/B$. In round numbers, its frequency discrimination is 10 times coarser or its time discrimination 1000 times coarser than those required by coherent detection schemes depending exclusively on frequency discrimination or time discrimination, respectively.

Exercise

What If the Noise and the Signal Are Interdependent?

In the examples cited up to now, it has been assumed that the amount of noise, which is represented by the variance of the observations, is independent of the signal. A look at Figure 5.4 shows that this is not universally true: Both for square-law and for linear rectifier detectors, the variance of the observation is greater when a signal is added to the noise than when the noise is examined without the signal. Under these circumstances, the expression

$$\frac{\mu_s - \mu_0}{\sigma}$$

is ambiguous, for we cannot tell which σ to use: σ_0, σ_s, or something between.

Show that if the threshold is set so there is a 50 per cent probability of missing the signal when it is present, then σ_0 is the one to use in the above formula.

Show that if the threshold is set for a 50 per cent probability of a false alarm when no signal is present, then σ_s is the appropriate one to use.

Consider the operational usefulness of both those threshold settings.

Exercise

Receiver Operating Characteristic (ROC)

The previous exercise shows that the effective signal-to-noise ratio may depend on the location of the threshold of the detector. If the probability of detection is plotted as a function of false-alarm probability for various threshold settings, the resulting curve is known as a *receiver operating characteristic*, or ROC. A set of ROC's for various input signal-to-noise ratios characterizes the sensitivity or detection performance of a receiver or demodulator. Figure 5.7 is a set of ROC's equivalent to the information in Table 4.1.

The scales are not linear: the scales are graduated in terms of the probability integrals $\Phi(x)$ and $\Phi(y)$, where

$$\Phi(z) = \frac{1}{\sqrt{2\pi}} \int_{-\infty}^{z} e^{-u^2/2} \, du$$

It is plotted on probability paper for two reasons: First, the scales are greatly expanded in the neighborhood of 0 and 1; and second, for most ordinary detectors the ROC's are a family of nearly straight, nearly parallel lines, which makes it easy to interpolate from a few points.

Show that for the case discussed in Section 4.2, whose results are tabulated in Table 4.1, the ROC's are precisely

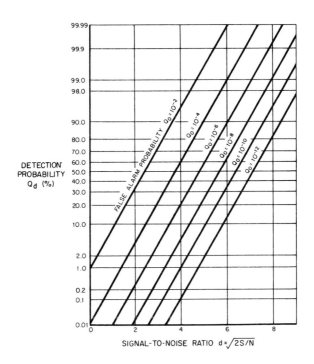

Figure 5.7   Receiver operating characteristic when a signal of known waveshape is detected by a correlation detector in white Gaussian noise.

parallel straight lines when plotted on probability paper like that of Figure 5.7.

Exercise

The Ambiguity Diagram

In discussing demodulation and detection, we have tacitly assumed that we are looking for, or at, one signal at most.

In real life, we may be looking for many signals at the same time, or we may be in doubt about where the signal is that we are looking for. If our equipment responded only to the "right" signal, and made no response to anything else, then it would be easy to sift out returns from multiple signals. However, theoretical and practical limitations prevent this: The response of the detector is not zero for every unwanted signal.

A particular case of interest is that in which a signal such as a radar return could arrive at any of a number of times, depending on the exact locations of particular targets, and with any of a number of Doppler shifts, characteristic of their respective speeds. The detector may be set to receive a return at a particular time and with a particular Doppler shift. Its response to other returns, as a function of time displacement and Doppler displacement, is called the ambiguity function of the detector. When an unwanted return appears at a range and speed where the detector ambiguity function is large, the detector is in danger of identifying it as a true target.

If the ambiguity function is represented graphically as contours or a multidimensional curved surface, it is called an ambiguity diagram.

A simple description of ambiguity diagrams and their use in sonar is contained in a paper by Stewart and Westerfield.* They show several examples. A more detailed discussion is found in Reference 9 of the Bibliography.

In many cases of practical interest, the variables in which the ambiguity function is expressed can be chosen so that the volume enclosed by the ambiguity diagram, conceived as a three-dimensional solid, is a system invariant independent of most of the system design variables. In many instances, this permits general conclusions which are intuitively easy to understand and have direct practical consequences.

* J. L. Stewart and E. C. Westerfield, "A Theory of Active Sonar Detection," *Proc. IRE*, *47*, 877–881 (1959).

6

Conclusion

Where, now, has this comparison of modulation and detection systems brought us? It has been shown that there is a minimum average energy required to transmit 1 bit of information in the presence of random noise of fixed intensity and uniform spectral distribution. The degree to which amplitude modulation, single-sideband modulation, frequency modulation, frequency modulation with feedback, and a particular frequency-band-limited noise-pulse modulation system approach the ideal has been estimated, and all were found to require 3 to 100 times more energy per bit than the ideal minimum. Detection of a signal in a noisy background, as in a radar, was viewed as a communication process, and it was found that the energy required per bit of effective information received is only slightly more than the ideal minimum.

Implicitly, we have seen how to encode an information-carrying signal of relatively narrow bandwidth and high signal-to-noise ratio in a new form having broad bandwidth and low signal-to-noise ratio. When the formula for channel capacity was developed, it became obvious at once that channels having a high signal-to-noise ratio used more power than is necessary to transmit their information. On the other hand, for a communication channel to be useful to the ultimate users, the received message must have a relatively high message-to-noise ratio, that is, the error rate must be low. In all of the more straightforward and naive ways of modulating and demodulating, the signal is so much like the message that to keep a high message-to-noise ratio, we must have a high signal-to-noise ratio.

The derivation we gave of the channel-capacity formula suggests one relatively complex way to signal through a noisy channel without introducing errors into the message: by using almost countless numbers of noiselike waveforms as an alphabet of digital signals. This solution to the problem is conceptually easy to handle, and on paper allows us to reach significant results. However, everyone seems to agree that this is an undesirable way to modulate and demodulate, or to code and decode, because it would require extremely complex equipment. Frequency modulation with feedback is a way of making a trade among bandwidth, power, and signal-to-noise ratio which realizes some of the possible gains. Practical digital coding devices are just being developed which allow further reduction in error rate or signal power, but at the expense of very complex terminal equipment.

Other advantages besides saving of transmitter power arise from the efficient use of a communication channel. For example, if we consider the efficient utilization of space in our signal space of $2WT$ dimensions, we realize that in signal space any noise is as good as any signal, and no signal is any better than any noise. Thus, we find that in such a context it is impossible to have especially obnoxious jamming signals. There is no more efficient signal for jamming than random noise, and we already know that under these circumstances the system can be designed to operate with a very low signal-to-noise ratio. We can see that to jam such a system successfully, we must put into the receiver more jamming power than signal power. This makes jamming costly.

There is another benefit from operating with a very low signal-to-noise ratio. If we can really work a communications system so that the signal power level is much lower than the noise power level, we introduce the possibility of signaling in such a way that it is hard to tell whether any signal is being transmitted at all. We can thus indirectly make the jamming problem more difficult again, for the jammer must first hunt around to find out where there is something to jam before he knows whether to waste his effort trying to jam it.

By looking at searching for the presence of a signal as a communication process, we have learned that there is a limit to the detectability of a single signal in a noise background, and that this limit is described in terms of the noise energy density and the received signal energy. The shape of the signal wave is not significant as long as it is fully known in advance to the detector. The process of measuring the correlation between the known signal waveform and the received wave is known as coherent detection. If the signal waveshape is not completely known, certain kinds of incoherent detection, which vary according to the degree of ignorance of the signal waveshape, are possible. The less that is known about the signal waveshape, the more signal energy is required to assure positive detection. If the signal is a single pulse or a burst of a sinusoidal wave, one can use very simple detectors which approach the theoretical limit of search performance. Many signals which at first contact appear to be quite specific, such as, for example, the acoustic signal resulting from the spoken sound "ee," do in fact vary over a wide range, and are correspondingly hard to detect reliably.

In summary, the ultimate limit to the rate of transmission of information in a noisy background, or to the detection of a signal in a noisy background, is primarily determined by the noise power density and the signal power or energy. To approach this theoretical limit, the receiver must have precise detailed knowledge of the possible waveshapes of the transmitted signal. In the absence of such knowledge, more signaling power or energy is required.

Bibliography

1. Fano, R. M., *Transmission of Information*, M.I.T. Press, Cambridge, Mass., 1961. A fundamental textbook on information theory for graduate students. If you want to know a great deal more than the present book can tell you, if your mathematical tools are bright and sharp, and if you are willing to work hard, you will probably want to read this.

2. Helstrom, C. W., *Statistical Theory of Detection*, Pergamon, London, 1960. A self-contained study of the aspects of information theory of importance to detection, with emphasis on the evolution of practical formulas and results.

3. Khinchin, A. I., *Mathematical Foundations of Information Theory*, translated by R. A. Silverman and M. D. Friedman, Dover, New York, 1957. A very clear and rigorous exposition and proof of the mathematical theorems underlying information theory.

4. Middleton, David, *An Introduction to Statistical Communication Theory*, McGraw-Hill, New York, 1960. This textbook attempts to reach practical end results while maintaining rigor. Where these goals conflict, the author is forced to exhaustive detail. It is a valuable comprehensive reference work.

5. Pierce, J. R., *Symbols, Signals, and Noise*, Harper, New York, 1961.

A nonmathematical account of some of the consequences and implications of information theory, illustrated with many applications and enlivened by the author's imaginative observations about many aspects of communication.

6. Pierce, J. R., and C. C. Cutler, *Interplanetary Communications*, contained in Advances in Space Science Vol. I, edited by F. I. Ordway III, Academic Press, New York, 1959. Contains a comparison of the channel capacity requirements of various signals and the capacities of various practical channels with a discussion of how these affect interplanetary communication system design.

7. Shannon, C. E., and W. Weaver, *A Mathematical Theory of Communication*, University of Illinois Press, Urbana, Ill., 1949. Reprints Shannon's 1948 paper of the same title in the *Bell System Technical Journal*, 27, 1948. The first detailed exposition of information theory with emphasis on communication, by one of its principal originators.

8. Wiener, N., *Cybernetics*, second edition, The M.I.T. Press, Cambridge, Mass., 1961. The first edition was the first comprehensive account of the theory of information, communication, and control with emphasis on prediction, filtering, and feedback control, as seen by one of the principal originators of the field. Substantial parts of the book are free from abstruse mathematics, and are interesting for their philosophical interpretation.

9. Woodward, P. M., *Probability and Information Theory, With Applications to Radar*, Pergamon, London, 1953. Somewhat more mathematical and a good deal more rigorous than the present volume. It gets additional vigor from being the authoritative statement of one of the early researchers in applications of information theory, written when the results were still a surprise.

10. Wozencraft, J. M., and B. Reiffen, *Sequential Decoding*, M.I.T. Press, Cambridge, Massachusetts, 1961. An exposition of a way of performing efficient digital coding for noisy discrete channels with relatively simple terminal equipment.

Index *

* Italicized page references indicate where the fullest explanation of a term is to be found.